Invisible Laws of Prosperity
Spiritual Secrets to Rewire Your Mind, Release Scarcity, and Manifest Lasting Wealth

Codex Occulto

© Copyright 2025 by Codex Occulto - All rights reserved.

This publication provides accurate and reliable information on the subject matter discussed. It is sold with the understanding that the publisher is not offering legal, accounting, or professional services. For such advice, consult a qualified expert.

No part of this document may be copied, reproduced, stored, or shared—electronically or in print—without written permission from the publisher. All rights reserved.

The content is presented as-is, with no guarantees. The publisher assumes no responsibility for any loss, damage, or consequences resulting from the use or misuse of the information provided.

Trademarks mentioned are the property of their respective owners and are used for identification purposes only. This publication is not affiliated with them.

All copyrights remain with their respective authors unless held by the publisher.

ISBN: 979-8-89965-378-0

Imprint: Staten House

Table of Content

THE RICH ARE NOT LUCKY. THEY'RE ALIGNED...7
THE 3 MYTHS THAT KEEP YOU BROKE...11
    MYTH #1: HARD WORK GUARANTEES WEALTH..11
    MYTH #2: WANTING MORE IS GREEDY OR WRONG..11
    MYTH #3: PROSPERITY IS RESERVED FOR THE LUCKY OR PRIVILEGED..........................12
    RELEASING THE MYTHS, RECLAIMING YOUR POWER..13
CHAPTER 2: PROSPERITY IS NOT MONEY (AT FIRST)...15
    THE FREQUENCY PRECEDES THE FORM...15
    FROM SCARCITY SCRIPTS TO ABUNDANCE STATES...16
    YOU ATTRACT WHO YOU ARE, NOT WHAT YOU WANT...17
    THE PARADOX OF PROSPERITY...17
CHAPTER 3: THE HIDDEN LAWS THAT ACTUALLY GOVERN ABUNDANCE................18
    THE LAW OF RESONANCE: YOU DON'T GET WHAT YOU WANT—YOU GET WHAT YOU ARE 19
    THE LAW OF EXPANSION: PROSPERITY FOLLOWS STRETCHING..19
    THE LAW OF CIRCULATION: WEALTH MUST MOVE TO MULTIPLY.....................................20
    THE LAW OF EMBODIMENT: ACT AS IF YOU ARE ALREADY IT..20
    LIVING WITH THE LAWS, NOT AGAINST THEM..21
CHAPTER 4: YOUR ENERGETIC SETPOINT: THE WEALTH THERMOSTAT....................23
    HOW THE THERMOSTAT IS INSTALLED..23
    NERVOUS SYSTEM SAFETY AND WEALTH..24
    RAISING THE SETPOINT THROUGH IDENTITY WORK..25
    ANCHORING THE NEW SETPOINT..25
CHAPTER 5: THE PROSPERITY PROGRAMMING YOU INHERITED...............................29
    THE ECHOES OF FAMILY BELIEFS..29
    CULTURAL AND COLLECTIVE CONDITIONING..30
    INHERITED TRAUMA AND FINANCIAL SAFETY..31
    REWRITING THE SCRIPT: FROM INHERITED TO INTENTIONAL..32
    YOU ARE NOT YOUR PROGRAMMING..33
CHAPTER 6: HOW TO REWIRE LACK AT THE CELLULAR LEVEL...................................35
    THE BRAIN-BODY CONNECTION AND FINANCIAL SAFETY..35
    REGULATING YOUR NERVOUS SYSTEM FOR ABUNDANCE...36
    CLEARING ENERGETIC RESIDUE FROM THE BODY..37

- Creating New Neural and Energetic Patterns.. 38
- You Were Never Broken—Just Unreprogrammed..39

Chapter 7: Language, Identity & Vibration.. 41
- Your Identity Is Your Wealth Ceiling... 41
- Vibration Is the Foundation of Manifestation....................................... 42
- Integrating the Three: Speak, Believe, Become................................... 43
- Who You Say You Are Is Who You Become... 44

Chapter 8: Emotions Are Energy – How to Transmute Fear into Flow..................... 44
- The Cost of Emotional Suppression... 45
- How to Transmute Fear into Flow.. 46
- Making Emotion Your Ally.. 47
- The Emotional Vibration of Wealth.. 47
- You Are a Channel, Not a Container.. 48

Chapter 9: The Law of Circulation – Why Hoarding Blocks Wealth..................... 52
- Hoarding Is a Symptom of Scarcity... 52
- Aligned Giving and Conscious Spending... 53
- The More You Give, the More You Become... 55

Chapter 10: The Law of Expansion – Why Stretching Attracts More.....................56
- Why Comfort Zones Become Cages..56
- Stretching Is the Currency of Abundance... 57
- From Expansion Anxiety to Expansion Mastery.................................. 58
- You Are Meant to Grow...59

Chapter 11: The Law of Embodiment – Be Before You Have................................. 62
- Who Are You Willing to Be?... 62
- Action From Identity, Not Insecurity... 63
- Living the Frequency Now.. 64
- Your Identity Shapes Your Reality.. 65
- Chapter 12: The Law of Resonance – Match What You Want............................ 66
- The Resonance You Don't Know You're Broadcasting......................... 66
- Coherence: Aligning Thoughts, Feelings, and Behavior......................67
- Becoming a Resonant Match for Your Next Level................................68
- Your Frequency Is Your Invitation... 69

Chapter 13: The $0 to Wealth Shift Plan.. 74
- Step 1: Mastering Your Internal State... 74

STEP 2: CREATE MICRO-MOMENTUM WITH ALIGNED ACTION.......................... 75
STEP 3: BUILD A NEW RELATIONSHIP WITH WEALTH.................................. 76
YOU'RE ALREADY IN MOTION... 78

CHAPTER 14: MONEY MANAGEMENT FOR ENERGY-SMART PEOPLE................ 80
RELEASING SHAME AND REBUILDING SAFETY..80
BUILDING A SYSTEM THAT HONORS YOUR ENERGY....................................81
EXPANDING YOUR CAPACITY TO HOLD MORE.. 83
BE THE STEWARD, NOT THE SERVANT..84

CHAPTER 15: THE PROSPERITY RITUALS THAT ACTUALLY WORK..................... 86
MORNING RITUALS: ACTIVATING THE FIELD... 86
EVENING RITUALS: CLOSING THE LOOP AND EXPANDING TRUST....................... 88
WEEKLY AND MONTHLY RITUALS: GROUNDING THE JOURNEY........................ 89
RITUALS MAKE YOU MAGNETIC... 90

CHAPTER 16: FROM SCARCITY TO OVERFLOW – THE 90-DAY RESET....................92
PHASE 1: CLEARING SCARCITY (DAYS 1–30)... 92
PHASE 2: BUILDING PROSPERITY HABITS (DAYS 31–60)................................ 94
PHASE 3: EXPANDING INTO OVERFLOW (DAYS 61–90)................................. 95
OVERFLOW IS THE OUTCOME OF ALIGNMENT... 96

CHAPTER 17: WEALTH WANTS TO FLOW THROUGH YOU................................ 102
RELEASING THE FEAR OF LOSS... 102
THE PURPOSE OF YOUR PROSPERITY... 103
BECOMING A SAFE AND SOVEREIGN CHANNEL... 104
YOU WERE MADE FOR THIS FLOW... 105

CHAPTER 18: HOW TO RECEIVE MORE WITHOUT GUILT OR BURNOUT.............. 108
YOUR NERVOUS SYSTEM AND THE CAPACITY TO HOLD MORE........................108
RELEASING GUILT AND DESERVINGNESS NARRATIVES................................. 109
CREATING SYSTEMS THAT SUPPORT OVERFLOW....................................... 110
RECEIVING IS THE BEGINNING, NOT THE END.. 112

CHAPTER 19: PROSPERITY & PURPOSE – ALIGNING MONEY WITH MEANING.....................113
DISCOVERING YOUR UNIQUE PURPOSE... 113
BRIDGING MONEY AND MEANING IN DAILY LIFE...114
PURPOSE-DRIVEN WEALTH IS SUSTAINABLE AND EXPANSIVE........................ 116

CHAPTER 20: THE INVISIBLE CODE OF THE TRULY ABUNDANT........................117
ABUNDANT PEOPLE TRUST BEFORE THEY SEE... 117

ABUNDANT PEOPLE CIRCULATE WITHOUT FEAR 118
ABUNDANT PEOPLE LET IDENTITY LEAD EVERYTHING 119
SEALING THE CODE: FROM KNOWLEDGE TO INTEGRATION 120

The Rich Are Not Lucky. They're Aligned.

If you've ever looked at someone living a life of ease, abundance, and freedom and thought, "Why not me?" — you're not alone. Most people have been conditioned to believe that wealth is a product of hustle, inherited privilege, or sheer dumb luck. But what if the truth is deeper, subtler, and far more empowering?
This book is here to tell you something radical: **the rich are not lucky. They're aligned**.
Aligned with what, exactly?
With invisible laws. With energy. With subconscious beliefs that support prosperity instead of sabotage. With a version of reality that responds not to effort, but to frequency. The truth is, the universe does not reward grind. It rewards resonance.
The reason some people seem to attract money, opportunity, support, and success effortlessly isn't because they work harder. It's because they are operating in harmony with the unseen rules of prosperity. They have, knowingly or not, tuned themselves to the right channel—one where abundance is normal, not miraculous.
The good news? You can do this too.
Prosperity is not reserved for a chosen few. It is a **state of being** you can cultivate. It starts within, not in your bank account. Before money shows up in your reality, it has to exist in your field. In your thoughts, your nervous system, your self-concept, your energy.
This book is your manual for mastering those inner dimensions. It's for those who are done with the struggle, the scarcity cycles, and the belief that they have to sacrifice their joy to be successful. It's for those ready to rewrite the rules—not the external ones, but the invisible ones that truly shape your experience.

We'll explore the hidden architecture behind real, sustainable wealth: the energetic patterns, emotional programs, and mental frameworks that either attract or repel prosperity. You'll learn how to identify and release inherited lack, how to raise your "wealth thermostat," and how to align with powerful laws like Circulation, Expansion, Embodiment, and Resonance.

You'll also get real-world tools and practices to bring these concepts down to earth—because theory without embodiment is just another form of distraction.

You don't need to force prosperity. You need to **become the kind of person it naturally flows to.**

Are you ready to stop chasing wealth and start attracting it?

Part I: Seeing the Invisible

The 3 Myths That Keep You Broke

Myth #1: Hard Work Guarantees Wealth
This is the myth most people hold onto the tightest, and it's also the one that causes the deepest disillusionment. We are taught from an early age that if you work hard, you'll be successful. It sounds noble. It sounds fair. And for a small segment of the population, it even seems to work. But for the vast majority, the equation doesn't add up.

The truth is, hard work without alignment creates burnout, not abundance.

If effort alone created prosperity, then every laborer, teacher, nurse, or single parent working multiple jobs would be swimming in wealth. Yet, many of these individuals live paycheck to paycheck. Meanwhile, others seem to create exponential success with minimal visible effort. Why? Because wealth is not a direct byproduct of time and labor. It is a byproduct of **frequency, belief, and alignment with unseen laws**.

Of course, effort matters. But effort in alignment is what creates flow. When you're aligned with who you truly are, with what brings you alive, and with the natural laws of expansion and circulation, you become magnetic. You work smarter, not harder. You begin to act from a place of inspiration, not desperation. And from that place, prosperity arrives with more ease.

If you're stuck in the cycle of grinding, ask yourself: *Is this effort creating expansion, or is it coming from fear?* Prosperity responds not to sacrifice, but to alignment.

Myth #2: Wanting More Is Greedy or Wrong
Many of us, consciously or not, carry the belief that desiring wealth is selfish, shallow, or spiritually corrupt. Maybe you grew up hearing phrases like "money doesn't grow on trees," "the love of money is the root of all evil," or "we're not the kind of people who get rich." These messages get embedded in your

subconscious and create a push-pull dynamic: you want more, but you also judge yourself for wanting more.

Here's the truth: **Desire is divine.**

Your desire for more wealth, freedom, or impact is not greed. It is guidance. It's your soul showing you the direction of your expansion. Wanting more doesn't make you less spiritual. In fact, when wealth flows into the hands of aligned, conscious, generous people, it can be a force for massive good.

When you suppress your desires, you also suppress your life force. You cut yourself off from your power. Abundance isn't just about getting things—it's about becoming more of who you really are. Wanting to create a beautiful, abundant, spacious life isn't wrong. It's natural.

So instead of judging your desires, listen to them. Let them guide you. Let them wake you up to the fact that more is possible. Because it is.

Myth #3: Prosperity Is Reserved for the Lucky or Privileged

Yes, privilege exists. And yes, systemic inequalities are real. But this myth does something dangerous: it convinces people that unless they were born into wealth or given special access, they are doomed to struggle. It takes away agency. It erodes self-trust.

The invisible truth is this: **while we can't control all external conditions, we can absolutely shift our internal state—and our internal state shapes our external reality.**

Prosperity responds to your inner frequency. And frequency isn't about social status. It's about how you feel, think, speak, and act. People from all walks of life, all backgrounds, all identities have found ways to access abundance by doing one essential thing: changing their energy.

When you shift from "Why them, not me?" to "If it's possible for them, it's possible for me too," you reclaim your power. You stop playing the game of comparison and start building your own field of abundance.

It doesn't happen overnight. But it begins with a choice: to believe that you are not an exception to prosperity. You are not the one person the universe forgot. You are not cursed, broken, or blocked forever. You are powerful. And you are being invited to learn how to play by new rules—the real rules.

Releasing the Myths, Reclaiming Your Power

These three myths aren't just harmless misunderstandings. They are energetic contracts. As long as you unconsciously agree with them, you'll keep manifesting scarcity, struggle, and self-doubt. The first step to breaking these patterns is **seeing them for what they are: inherited limitations**.

You don't need to hustle harder. You don't need to feel guilty for wanting more. You don't need to believe that wealth is only for the chosen few.

You need to start telling yourself a new story.

The truth is, prosperity is not just possible for you—it's natural. But you must begin to align your energy, thoughts, emotions, and identity with that truth. The rest of this book will show you how.

But first, let's get clear on what prosperity really is—because it's not just money.

Chapter 2: Prosperity Is Not Money (At First)

Ask the average person to define prosperity, and they'll most likely mention wealth, luxury, or financial security. Maybe they'll picture a mansion on a hill, a luxury car in the driveway, or a bulging bank account. But here's a truth that might surprise you: **prosperity doesn't begin with money.** It begins with how you feel.

Money is a **symptom**, not the source. It's a mirror reflecting your internal relationship to abundance, worthiness, and trust. If you think prosperity is only about how much cash you have, you're playing the game backwards. People who are truly prosperous radiate something long before they get rich. They feel a sense of fullness, gratitude, and possibility inside them—regardless of their current income.

This shift in definition is crucial. If you keep measuring prosperity by external markers, you'll always feel like you're behind. But when you begin to feel prosperous internally—before the money arrives—you start to align with the very frequency that attracts abundance in the first place.

The feeling of prosperity precedes its physical form. That's not spiritual fluff; it's energetic fact.

The Frequency Precedes the Form

Everything in the universe operates on frequency. Your thoughts, your emotions, your beliefs—they all emit a vibrational signal. This signal communicates to the world what you're available for. Think of it like a tuning fork: if your internal signal is one of fear, lack, or unworthiness, that's the kind of experience you'll magnetize. On the flip side, when your signal is one of abundance, joy, and trust, you become a match for more prosperous experiences.

So the question becomes: **Are you vibrating in lack, or in wealth—even if your wallet is thin?**

This is why people who feel rich before they are rich tend to attract wealth more easily. They're not faking it. They're embodying a feeling state that generates real-world shifts. And when your nervous system learns to feel safe in abundance—before it tangibly arrives—you start noticing new opportunities, making bolder choices, and welcoming support instead of sabotaging it.

In other words, **you don't become rich and then feel abundant. You feel abundant, and then you become rich.**

This isn't about lying to yourself or pretending you're not struggling. It's about recognizing that you have power over your internal state—and that internal state is the true engine of your external life.

From Scarcity Scripts to Abundance States

Most people live inside mental and emotional patterns inherited from childhood, culture, or past trauma. These patterns often operate unconsciously and sound something like this:

- "I have to work harder to deserve more."
- "I'll never get ahead no matter what I do."
- "There's never enough to go around."
- "Wealthy people must have done something unethical."

These internal scripts create a baseline feeling of scarcity—a constant sense of not enough. Not enough time, not enough support, not enough self-worth. And from that place, even when money does show up, it disappears quickly, gets blocked, or comes with guilt and burnout.

To shift into prosperity, you must rewrite your internal scripts. This means choosing to cultivate feelings of *sufficiency, gratitude, expansion, and ease*—not as a reward, but as a foundation.

This might look like:

- Practicing gratitude for what you already have, not as a performance, but as an energetic anchor.
- Visualizing and *feeling into* a future where your needs are met with ease.

- Choosing to focus on how resourceful, creative, and supported you already are—even in moments of challenge.

These practices help your nervous system stabilize in a new baseline: one of prosperity, not panic. And once you've established that internal shift, your external world begins to reflect it.

You Attract Who You Are, Not What You Want

This is one of the most confronting truths in the prosperity journey: **you don't get what you want—you get what you are.**

Many people walk around with long lists of what they wish for—more money, more clients, a better job, a bigger house. But underneath that wish list is often a deep feeling of lack. And that lack becomes the dominant signal the universe responds to.

Wanting, in and of itself, doesn't create prosperity. In fact, excessive wanting often stems from a subconscious belief that you are incomplete without the thing you desire. That belief emits a frequency of separation, not attraction.

But when you shift from **wanting** to **being**, everything changes.

You begin to ask:

- How would the prosperous version of me walk into this room?
- How would I speak, act, and make decisions if I knew abundance was inevitable?
- What would I allow myself to receive, without guilt?

You stop chasing money and start embodying wealth.

And the more consistently you hold that vibration, the more naturally money flows to you—not as a goal, but as a byproduct of who you've become.

This is what spiritual teachers, mystics, and modern coaches have all been trying to communicate in their own language: **prosperity is not something you achieve. It's something you align with.**

The Paradox of Prosperity

Here's the paradox that most people resist: in order to attract more, you have to stop needing more.

That doesn't mean giving up desire—it means detaching from desperation. It means choosing to live and move from a place of sufficiency, even while you're growing. It means deciding that you are already enough, and acting like someone who is trustworthy with wealth—not someone waiting to be rescued by it.

When you stop trying to prove your worthiness, prosperity comes faster.

When you stop clinging to outcomes, opportunities start showing up.

When you stop looking for money to validate your value, you begin to *embody* value—and value always attracts wealth.

This doesn't mean you stop working, dreaming, or growing. It means you stop outsourcing your power to numbers in a bank account. You stop measuring your prosperity by how many zeroes you have and start measuring it by how aligned, alive, and supported you feel.

Because here's the real secret: when you feel like a prosperous person, you start behaving like one. And the world rearranges itself around that identity.

Chapter 3: The Hidden Laws That Actually Govern Abundance

In this chapter, we'll explore four of these laws: the Law of Resonance, the Law of Expansion, the Law of Circulation, and the Law of Embodiment. These are not steps in a formula—they are conditions of alignment. You don't control them, but you do cooperate with them. Once you begin to live in harmony with these principles, what used to feel like force becomes flow.

The Law of Resonance: You Don't Get What You Want—You Get What You Are

Everything in existence vibrates. Your thoughts, your emotions, your memories, your beliefs—all emit frequencies. The Law of Resonance states that like attracts like. What you're broadcasting is mirrored back to you in the form of people, opportunities, patterns, and results.

This means you can't simply "want" more money or "wish" for success. If your dominant vibration is fear, scarcity, or shame, those are the experiences you'll magnetize—regardless of your conscious intentions. Resonance always responds to your core frequency, not your wishlist.

If your life seems stuck, it's not because the universe is withholding something from you. It's because you're in resonance with your current level of experience. This can be hard to accept. But it's also incredibly empowering—because it means that by changing your inner state, you change what you're available for.

Want to attract more wealth? Then cultivate the inner state of someone who feels wealthy now—not in the future, but today. How would you think, speak, walk, or act if you truly believed in your worth and sufficiency?

The Law of Expansion: Prosperity Follows Stretching

Nature expands. The universe expands. Your soul, too, is wired to expand. The Law of Expansion says that the more you grow, the more you can receive. The more space you create within yourself—emotionally, energetically, spiritually—the more prosperity has room to enter.

But expansion isn't always comfortable. It often requires letting go of what's familiar—comfort zones, old identities, inherited beliefs. It may mean saying yes to risks, conversations, or investments that feel slightly outside your current self-concept. And that discomfort? That's the stretching.

A common reason people unconsciously block prosperity is because they want the rewards of expansion without the process. They want more without becoming more. But abundance only flows into structures that can hold it. If you want to hold more, you must become more spacious.

You expand by showing up to life with curiosity instead of control, by saying yes to growth even when you're uncertain, and by trusting that your nervous system can adapt to greater good.

The Law of Circulation: Wealth Must Move to Multiply

Stagnation is the enemy of abundance. Money, like energy, must move. The Law of Circulation teaches that prosperity is not something to hoard—it's something to flow. When you hold too tightly to money out of fear, you choke the very current that would replenish you. Circulation isn't about reckless spending; it's about conscious movement.

Think of money like breath. You don't inhale and then try to keep it in your lungs forever. You exhale, and in doing so, make room for more. The same applies to wealth. When you give, invest, support, tip, and spend with trust instead of tension, you participate in the natural cycle of giving and receiving. The universe notices—and responds.

Circulation applies to more than money. It includes your gifts, your attention, your time, your creativity. When you hoard these things, you operate from scarcity. But when you share them generously, you activate a feedback loop of generosity from the world around you.

You don't need to empty your bank account to practice circulation. You simply need to make decisions from abundance, not contraction. Ask yourself: Am I moving this money from a place of faith or from fear? One grows your field. The other shrinks it.

The Law of Embodiment: Act As If You Are Already It

If the Law of Resonance aligns your vibration, the Law of Embodiment aligns your identity. Embodiment means you don't just "think" prosperous thoughts—you become the person who lives in them. You act, decide, and behave from your future self, not your past patterns.

Most people believe in the sequence: Have → Do → Be. Once I have the money, I'll do the things, and then I'll feel worthy, peaceful, and free. But embodiment flips the order. Be → Do → Have. When you become the person who trusts, invests, and expands—even before the outcome—you naturally take aligned action, which then produces results.

This law requires boldness. It means showing up as the version of yourself who already knows they are supported by life. Not pretending or faking—it's about tuning into that version of you that already exists in potential and living from that place today.

What would a wealthy you say yes to? What would they say no to? How would they manage time, money, rest, or boundaries? Embodiment is not a performance. It's a remembering. You're not becoming someone else—you're removing the parts of you that forgot who you already are.

You don't have to wait to be wealthy to start living like someone who values themselves. Start today. Embody prosperity, and the rest follows.

Living with the Laws, Not Against Them

The truth is, these laws are already working in your life, whether you're conscious of them or not. They don't turn off when you ignore them—they simply reflect your current state. Most people struggle with prosperity not because they're lazy or flawed, but because they're operating unconsciously within a system they don't understand.

Now you understand.

You can begin to live differently—not by hustling harder, but by aligning more deeply. The moment you shift your vibration, your identity, your willingness to grow, and your generosity of circulation, you become a new channel for abundance.

These laws are not theoretical. They're practical. You'll see their effects when you apply them—not perfectly, but consistently.

You'll feel more supported, more inspired, and more available for the kind of wealth that uplifts, not depletes.

And as you continue to integrate these principles, you'll come face-to-face with another powerful truth: your prosperity will always be capped by your inner ceiling. That ceiling isn't made of glass. It's made of belief, trauma, nervous system regulation, and self-worth.

Chapter 4: Your Energetic Setpoint: The Wealth Thermostat

You might have had moments in life when everything seemed to be going right. Money was flowing, opportunities were showing up, and success felt within reach. Then, almost inexplicably, things slipped. An unexpected expense drained your savings. You lost the momentum. The deal fell through. And you found yourself back at your previous "normal."

This pattern isn't a coincidence. It's the effect of something subtle but powerful: your energetic setpoint.

Just as your body has a temperature it tries to maintain—around 98.6 degrees Fahrenheit—your mind and nervous system also have a setpoint for wealth, joy, and expansion. This is your **wealth thermostat**. It determines how much abundance you feel safe holding.

The key to lasting prosperity is not just to manifest more, but to *raise the thermostat*. To teach your system that abundance is your new normal. That safety and wealth can coexist. That overflow isn't a threat—it's your birthright.

How the Thermostat Is Installed

Various messages shape your beliefs about money, work, success, and worth.

You might have absorbed ideas like:
- "We can't afford that."
- "Money doesn't grow on trees."
- "Rich people are greedy."
- "Don't ask for too much."
- "If you want something, you have to earn it—twice."

These ideas didn't just form beliefs. They wired a *feeling* into your body—a visceral reaction to receiving, spending, asking, or having "too much." Over time, these feelings solidify into your setpoint.

As an adult, this means you may find yourself sabotaging opportunities, undercharging for your work, procrastinating on financial tasks, or avoiding growth—even when you consciously want more. These aren't failures of willpower. They're protective mechanisms from a system that doesn't feel safe with more.

Your job now is to become aware of the setpoint—and to start rewiring it.

Nervous System Safety and Wealth

Here's a fundamental truth: *Your nervous system always chooses familiarity over success if success feels threatening.*

You can tell yourself you want to make six figures, or launch a business, or invest boldly. But if your body associates wealth with rejection, loss, stress, or unworthiness, it will activate internal brakes. You may freeze. You may distract yourself. You may pick a fight, delay a decision, or downsize your dream without fully realizing it.

This is your wealth thermostat doing its job—bringing you "back" to the emotional temperature that feels safe.

To raise your setpoint, you must work with your body, not just your mind. This is where true transformation happens.

You begin by creating safety in your nervous system for larger amounts of money, greater visibility, deeper trust, and more powerful self-expression. You start with what feels slightly stretchy but not overwhelming.

For example:
- Imagine receiving $1,000 unexpectedly. What happens in your body? Do you feel joy, guilt, tension, skepticism?
- Imagine doubling your rates. Do you feel empowered—or exposed?
- Imagine getting everything you want. Do you feel expansive—or anxious?

These internal responses show you where your thermostat is set. They're not judgments—they're clues.

Bit by bit, your system will learn that it's safe to grow.

Raising the Setpoint Through Identity Work

One of the most effective ways to raise your energetic setpoint is to upgrade your self-concept—your identity.

You will never consistently outperform the story you believe about who you are.

So the question becomes: *Who are you when you're truly prosperous?*

You begin by imagining and embodying that version of yourself, not as a fantasy, but as a reference point. What are their habits? Their boundaries? Their energy? How do they talk to themselves? How do they move through the world?

Once you have a vision of that version of you, begin to act accordingly in small, doable ways. You don't need to leap into a new life overnight. But you can start aligning your choices with the person you're becoming.

Say no where you used to overgive. Speak up where you used to stay silent. Rest instead of rushing. Raise your standards. Upgrade your environment. Choose from faith, not fear.

This isn't about pretending. It's about building new patterns—neural, emotional, and energetic—that support a higher setpoint.

You are becoming someone who is safe with abundance. Someone who can receive without guilt. Someone who can grow without shrinking.

As your identity evolves, your setpoint rises.

Anchoring the New Setpoint

Raising your wealth thermostat is not a one-time event. It's a process of *integration*. That means embodying the new level of wealth not just when things are going well, but also when challenges arise.

One of the most powerful ways to anchor your new setpoint is through repetition and regulation.

Repetition means consistently practicing the thoughts, emotions, and behaviors of your prosperous self—even when you don't "feel" it. It's showing up for the new reality until it becomes your default.

Regulation means tending to your nervous system so that expansion feels safe. This could include:
- Breathwork and somatic practices to soothe overwhelm.
- Emotional release to clear old trauma.
- Restoring safety through movement, music, or time in nature.
- Therapy, coaching, or mentorship to support your evolution.

When you combine repetition and regulation, you not only raise the setpoint—you *maintain* it.

You Are the Thermostat

Here's the ultimate shift: you are not just adjusting to life—you are setting the temperature.

Your life reflects what your system believes is possible and safe. By raising the setpoint, you raise the quality of opportunities, relationships, and wealth that come into your field.

You don't need to fight for abundance. You just need to *become someone who's ready for it.*

PART II: RECODING YOUR FIELD

Chapter 5: The Prosperity Programming You Inherited

Wealth Is Not Just Personal—It's Generational
You were born into a world already filled with ideas about money, value, and success. Long before you could form your own opinions, you absorbed the energy and beliefs of the people around you. In this way, your relationship with prosperity didn't begin with your first paycheck or your first budgeting app—it began in the air you breathed as a child.

Wealth consciousness is not created in a vacuum. It's passed down through stories, behaviors, warnings, and even silence. These inherited patterns are so embedded that most of us mistake them for personality traits or "just how things are." But in truth, what you inherited isn't who you are—it's just what you've been programmed to believe.

To create real, lasting prosperity, you must understand this programming—not to blame anyone, but to gain power over what you've unconsciously agreed to. Because when you see the script, you can finally rewrite it.

The Echoes of Family Beliefs

Think back to your childhood. What was the emotional atmosphere around money? Was it a source of tension, shame, pride, secrecy, or power? Did people speak about it openly and calmly—or was it avoided, fought over, or judged?

Maybe you heard things like:
- "We can't afford that."
- "Don't waste money."
- "Money doesn't buy happiness."
- "Rich people are selfish."
- "You have to work twice as hard to get half as much."

These phrases, even if spoken casually, became part of your internal belief system. Even if your adult mind rejects them, your subconscious often still operates by their rules. Why? Because your subconscious is designed to preserve what is familiar—not what is empowering.

Your nervous system remembers the emotional charge that surrounded money. If asking for things brought conflict, you might now fear asking for a raise. If generosity was punished, you might struggle to give or receive. If wealth was associated with abandonment or stress, you might sabotage it when it comes close.

These patterns aren't about logic—they're about protection. Your system learned that staying in the financial emotional range of your family equals safety. That's why, without conscious intervention, you may find yourself repeating the same financial experiences, even if they no longer serve you.

Recognizing these echoes is not about criticizing your parents or caretakers. They were doing the best they could with what they inherited. But awareness gives you choice. And choice is the beginning of freedom.

Cultural and Collective Conditioning

Beyond your family, you were also shaped by the broader cultural context in which you were raised. Every society carries implicit messages about what it means to be "successful," who deserves wealth, and how prosperity should be pursued—or punished.

You may have internalized beliefs like:
- "Struggle is noble."
- "Success only comes with sacrifice."
- "You must choose between doing good and getting rich."
- "Artists, healers, or spiritual people shouldn't care about money."
- "Wealth is for other people—not people like me."

These messages are reinforced through media, school, religion, and even casual conversations. Over time, they become part of the invisible architecture of your worldview.

For example, if your culture idolizes hard work but mocks ease, you may feel guilty when abundance comes without struggle. If your community equates wealth with corruption, you may unconsciously push money away to stay "good." If your religion framed poverty as purity, your higher self may feel in conflict with financial gain.

These belief systems operate under the surface, but they shape everything. They influence how much you allow yourself to earn, ask for, spend, and enjoy. They create inner resistance when you try to "level up"—because doing so would break the collective agreement you grew up inside.

To rewrite your prosperity programming, you must begin to challenge these cultural myths. Not with anger, but with curiosity. Ask yourself: *Is this belief truly mine? Or is it something I absorbed and never questioned?* The answers will start to crack the code.

Inherited Trauma and Financial Safety

One of the most overlooked aspects of prosperity programming is inherited trauma—not just emotional trauma, but financial trauma passed down through generations.

Perhaps your grandparents fled war or grew up in the Depression. Maybe your parents experienced bankruptcy, addiction, or chronic instability. Even if these events weren't spoken about directly, they were felt—and those feelings shaped your sense of financial safety.

Trauma doesn't just pass through stories. It passes through behaviors, coping mechanisms, and unspoken fears. It can look like:

- Hoarding money or never feeling like there's enough.
- Fear of spending even when you have plenty.
- Under-earning to avoid attention or envy.
- Avoiding financial conversations altogether.
- Feeling anxious any time you receive or gain more.

These are not random behaviors. They are trauma responses—attempts by your system to stay safe based on what it learned survival required.

What's powerful is that trauma, once seen, can be healed. You don't have to stay loyal to a legacy of struggle. You can honor your ancestors while choosing a new pattern. You can thank your nervous system for protecting you—and gently show it that you are safe to create a new reality.

This is why prosperity work is not just mindset work. It's *healing work*. It's about returning to your body and telling it, over and over: "It's okay to receive. It's safe to have. I'm allowed to want more."

Rewriting the Script: From Inherited to Intentional

Once you've identified the programming you inherited, the next step is to consciously choose what you want to believe instead. This doesn't happen overnight—but it does happen with intention.

Begin by writing out the dominant beliefs you've carried about money. Don't filter them—just let them pour out. Then next to each one, write a new belief that feels slightly more empowering. Don't jump to extreme affirmations your system won't believe. Choose bridge beliefs—statements that stretch you, but still feel within reach.

For example:
- "Money always runs out" becomes "I'm learning to create consistent inflow."
- "I'm bad with money" becomes "I'm becoming someone who manages money with care."
- "Wealth is not for people like me" becomes "Wealth is becoming part of my story."

Next, begin acting in small ways that reflect these new beliefs. Maybe you open a savings account, ask for support, or celebrate a win without minimizing it. These micro-actions create a feedback loop: new beliefs → new behavior → new outcomes → reinforced belief.

Each time you choose differently, you loosen the grip of the past. Each time you act from intention rather than inheritance, you break the cycle.

Eventually, the inherited script fades—and a new narrative begins.

You Are Not Your Programming

Perhaps the most important truth of all is this: *You are not your programming. You are the author now.*

What you absorbed was real—but it doesn't have to define you. You are allowed to choose a new reality. You are allowed to feel safe with wealth. You are allowed to expand beyond what your lineage ever imagined.

This chapter is about awareness, not shame. It's about noticing what shaped you so you can shape something better. It's about becoming the one who ends the old story and begins the new one—not just for yourself, but for everyone who comes after.

The programming isn't permanent. You're already rewriting it. Let's keep going.

Chapter 6: How to Rewire Lack at the Cellular Level

You've probably heard the phrase, "Change your thoughts, change your life." And while mindset work has value, it often hits a wall—especially when it comes to money and prosperity. Why? Because the root of lack is not just in your thoughts. It's in your *nervous system*. In your body. In the emotional memory stored in your cells.

You can write affirmations until your hand cramps. You can recite mantras in the mirror every morning. But if your body is still carrying fear, trauma, or survival-based programming, those affirmations won't land. Your body will override your best intentions, because it doesn't feel *safe* with wealth.

To truly shift from scarcity to prosperity, you must go beyond positive thinking. You must engage your *entire system*—brain, body, and energy field. This is the work of *cellular rewiring*. It's not about forcing yourself to believe something new. It's about creating an environment inside you where new beliefs can *actually live*.

In this chapter, we'll explore the intersection of neuroscience, emotional regulation, and energetic healing—and how these tools can work together to release the imprint of lack, so you can become someone who naturally aligns with abundance.

The Brain-Body Connection and Financial Safety

Let's start with the brain. Your brain's primary job is not to make you rich or successful. Its job is to keep you *alive*. It does this by scanning for danger, predicting outcomes based on past experiences, and creating behaviors that minimize perceived threats.

Unfortunately, if you've ever associated wealth with danger—rejection, judgment, loss, overwhelm—then your brain may flag prosperity itself as a threat. It doesn't care that you want more money. It only cares that in the past, "more" meant stress, conflict, or pressure. So it protects you the only way it knows how: by keeping you small.

This isn't self-sabotage. It's self-protection.

What's more, the brain and body are in constant communication. Every thought you have triggers a chemical response in your body. Every emotion sends a signal that reinforces certain neural pathways. This is how patterns become hardwired. And this is why you can feel stuck in lack, even when you know better intellectually.

The key to change is *neuroplasticity*—your brain's ability to form new connections. But for neuroplasticity to work, your body has to feel *safe enough* to receive new information. Safety is the foundation. Without it, your system rejects change—even if it's positive.

So before you "think rich," you must teach your body it's safe to *be rich*. That's where nervous system work comes in.

Regulating Your Nervous System for Abundance

Your nervous system is the operating system behind everything. It controls your fight-or-flight response, your emotional regulation, your ability to connect, your sense of confidence, and your capacity to receive. It stores unresolved trauma and determines how much stress—or joy—you can handle.

When your nervous system is dysregulated, abundance feels overwhelming. Receiving feels unsafe. Expansion feels exhausting. You may find yourself freezing, procrastinating, avoiding, or overworking—not because you're lazy or unmotivated, but because your system is trying to stay in its comfort zone.

Rewiring lack begins with creating *regulation*. This means teaching your nervous system how to remain calm, centered, and open—even when you're experiencing more visibility, more income, more responsibility, or more joy.

Here are several ways to begin regulating your system for prosperity:

Breathwork: Deep, conscious breathing activates the parasympathetic nervous system, which signals safety to the body. When you feel triggered around money (a bill, a price increase, a big opportunity), pause. Breathe deeply. Inhale for four counts, hold for four, exhale for six. This simple act grounds your energy and resets your physiology.

Movement: Scarcity often creates tension in the body. Shake it out. Walk. Stretch. Dance. Move energy through your system. The more freely you move, the more freely energy—including financial energy—can flow through you.

Somatic Tracking: Instead of escaping discomfort, learn to sit with it. If fear arises, ask yourself: *Where do I feel this in my body?* Place your attention there. Breathe into it. Don't judge it. Just witness it. This practice teaches your system that you can handle intensity without shutting down.

Resourcing: Recall moments when you felt safe, supported, and held—financially or otherwise. Let those memories fill your body. This "resourcing" practice creates a baseline of safety, which allows for greater expansion.

Co-regulation: We heal faster in connection. Spend time with people who embody calm, wealth, and generosity. Their nervous systems will "speak" to yours and help retrain your internal state.

As you practice regulation, your body begins to associate abundance not with danger, but with safety. And from that state, true change is possible.

Clearing Energetic Residue from the Body

Beyond the brain and nervous system, your energy field also holds imprints of past experiences—especially unprocessed emotions related to lack, shame, or fear. These energetic blocks can weigh you down, even if you're doing all the "right" things.

Clearing this residue requires energetic hygiene. Just like you wouldn't go weeks without a shower, your energy needs cleansing—especially if you've spent years absorbing scarcity from your environment.

Here are a few methods to begin clearing energetically:

Grounding: Spend time barefoot in nature. Visualize roots growing from your feet into the earth. This grounds your energy and discharges static fear or anxiety.

Energetic Scanning: Sit quietly. Visualize a light scanning your body from head to toe. Notice any "stuck" areas—places that feel heavy, tense, or dark. Imagine those areas being bathed in light and cleared gently.

Sound and Frequency: Sound has a direct impact on the body's vibrational field. Listen to high-frequency music, tuning forks, or mantra chanting. These vibrations help break up stagnant patterns.

Water Rituals

Baths, showers, or simply rinsing your hands with intention can serve as energetic reset points. Imagine lack or fear washing off you and going down the drain.

Visualization: magine your energetic field expanding. See yourself surrounded by light. Visualize money and opportunity flowing toward you and through you with ease. Let it feel real in your body—not just your mind.

The more you clear, the more space you make for new, empowering energy to anchor into your field.

Creating New Neural and Energetic Patterns

Once your system is safe and your energy is clear, you can begin *installing new programming*. This isn't about forcing a new reality—it's about *inviting* it.

The brain learns through repetition and emotion. So combine both.

Use Affirmations with Feeling: Don't just say, "I am abundant." Say it while breathing deeply, smiling, and standing tall. Let your body feel it.

Rehearse Your Future Self: Daily, spend a few minutes imagining your prosperous self. What are they wearing? How do they move? What decisions do they make? Practice *being* them now.

Anchor Success: Every time something goes right, *celebrate*. Anchor the feeling into your body. Say, "This is what success feels like. This is safe."

Create Micro-Wins: Set small, doable goals and meet them. These create positive feedback loops that reinforce your new identity.

Be Consistent: The brain needs consistency more than intensity. Show up daily. Even two minutes of presence rewires faster than occasional effort.

Over time, your body, mind, and field start to operate as if abundance is already here—because to them, it *is*.

You Were Never Broken—Just Unreprogrammed

Rewiring lack at the cellular level doesn't mean fixing yourself. It means *freeing* yourself. Beneath the fear, shame, and old programming, your original blueprint is intact. You were born whole, powerful, and capable of receiving.

You don't need to become someone else. You need to remember who you were before lack took over your system.

This is not just about money. It's about your capacity to hold life, love, joy, creativity, and power. It's about expanding what your system believes is possible—and safe.

Chapter 7: Language, Identity & Vibration

Language is not just a way to communicate—it's a tool of creation. Every word you speak sends out a vibrational signal that reflects your internal world and shapes your external experience. Your words are spells. They are declarations of belief, of expectation, and of identity.

Think about how often we casually curse ourselves with phrases like:
- "I'm broke."
- "I can't afford that."
- "That's out of my league."
- "I'm not good with money."
- "Things never work out for me."

These might feel like harmless expressions, but they're more powerful than they appear. They are energetic contracts. Every time you say them, you reinforce a reality of limitation.

You're not just describing your life—you're prescribing it.

On the flip side, consider the impact of shifting your language to reflect possibility and power:
- "I'm learning to manage money well."
- "I choose to spend mindfully."
- "I am available for new opportunities."
- "Wealth is growing around and within me."

Notice how these phrases feel in your body. They invite expansion. They point toward a version of you that is capable, open, and aligned with abundance.

Your words calibrate your vibration. They can either anchor you to scarcity or attune you to overflow. If you want to change your financial reality, start by changing the way you talk about it.

Your Identity Is Your Wealth Ceiling

While words influence your vibration, identity determines its range.

If you see yourself as someone who's "bad with money," "always catching up," or "just not meant for wealth," those identities will quietly sabotage your growth. You may receive windfalls and lose them. You may reach new heights and panic. You may shrink opportunities to fit the smaller story you've been living inside.

It's not because you don't deserve more. It's because your *current identity doesn't recognize more as safe.*

To break free, you must evolve your self-image—not by pretending, but by remembering.

Start by asking yourself:

- Who have I believed I had to be to stay safe, loved, or accepted?
- What roles or labels have I taken on that no longer serve me?
- What identity would a truly prosperous version of me hold?

This might mean releasing identities like "the selfless one," "the underdog," "the struggler," "the saver," or "the survivor." These roles may have protected you. They may have been praised. But if they are keeping you small, it's time to outgrow them.

Begin crafting a new identity—one that reflects your capacity, not your past. Give yourself permission to try on phrases like:

- "I am a powerful creator of wealth."
- "I am a generous receiver."
- "I am someone who makes money with integrity and ease."
- "I am worthy of thriving, not just surviving."

Repeat them. Embody them. Take small actions that reinforce them. Let the new identity root in your nervous system through repetition, embodiment, and practice.

Vibration Is the Foundation of Manifestation

At the root of both language and identity is something even more fundamental: *vibration.* Your vibration is the energetic frequency you emit through your emotions, thoughts, intentions, and actions.

You can think of vibration like a radio signal. Whatever station you're tuned to determines what you hear. Tune into lack, fear, and resentment, and you attract more of the same. Tune into gratitude, trust, and sufficiency, and you start receiving in a different way.

The question isn't just "What do I want?" but "What am I tuned to?"

Start noticing what you broadcast in your everyday life. Your tone, your emotions, your stories, your self-talk—they all signal your dominant frequency.

This means choosing your frequency with care. It means honoring your feelings while still anchoring into a deeper truth—that you are worthy.

Practices that help you raise your vibration include:
- Gratitude journaling (focus on feelings, not just lists).
- Movement and dance to shift stagnant energy.
- Breathwork and meditation to recalibrate your system.
- Speaking affirmations aloud with emotion.
- Spending time with people who embody high-frequency energy.
- Engaging with beauty, creativity, and nature.

Every time you raise your vibration, even slightly, you become a match for new outcomes.

Integrating the Three: Speak, Believe, Become

When you bring language, identity, and vibration into alignment, you create unstoppable momentum. You're no longer fighting yourself. You're reinforcing your truth across every level of your being.

Here's how it works in practice:
1. **Language** is the daily reinforcement. It trains your mind and informs your energy.
2. **Identity** is the framework. It determines what feels possible and normal to you.
3. **Vibration** is the atmosphere. It's the energetic soil in which your results grow.

You don't need to be perfect. You just need to be consistent. Start small:
- Catch yourself when you speak scarcity—and reframe it.
- Choose one new belief about who you are becoming—and act accordingly.
- Tend to your energy daily, like you would a garden.

Over time, this alignment compounds. You stop chasing wealth and start living in the frequency where wealth finds you.

Who You Say You Are Is Who You Become

You are the narrator of your life. The words you speak, the identity you embody, and the energy you emit are the pen, paper, and ink of your story. Every day, you have the chance to edit the script—not by force, but by resonance.

If you want to be prosperous, speak like someone who already is. If you want to hold more wealth, become someone who believes they are worthy of it. If you want to create overflow, cultivate the energy of gratitude, courage, and generosity now—not someday, but today.

Chapter 8: Emotions Are Energy – How to Transmute Fear into Flow

You've been taught to believe that emotions are personal, internal experiences—messy things to manage or hide. But in the realm of energetic prosperity, emotions are something else entirely: they are *currents of energy* that shape your vibration, influence your nervous system, and magnetize (or repel) abundance.

Your emotions are creative forces.

So if you want to become a match for flow, ease, and prosperity, you can't just "think rich." You must *feel* rich. And not in a fake-it way. In a deep, embodied, cellular way. This means acknowledging and transforming the emotional patterns that keep you stuck in lack—especially fear.

Fear is the root of scarcity. It's the anchor behind procrastination, under-earning, avoidance, and self-sabotage. But fear itself is not the enemy. It only becomes a block when you resist it. When you learn to *feel* your fear, you free it. When you transmute fear into movement, you unlock flow.

The Cost of Emotional Suppression

Most people walk around carrying years—sometimes decades—of suppressed emotion. Feelings that weren't allowed to be expressed in childhood. Grief that had no space. Rage that had to be swallowed. Shame that was internalized instead of healed.

These unprocessed emotions don't disappear. They go underground—into your nervous system, your muscles, your subconscious mind. There, they calcify into patterns: avoidance, defensiveness, anxiety, perfectionism, overworking, or numbness. These patterns don't just affect your well-being. They affect your ability to *receive*.

Receiving requires openness. But suppressed emotion closes the channel.

You might think you're protecting yourself by staying "strong" and ignoring fear. But what you're really doing is blocking flow. Emotions are like water. If they don't move, they stagnate. And stagnation is the opposite of prosperity.

Here are a few common signs that emotional suppression is affecting your wealth field:

- You freeze or procrastinate on decisions involving money.
- You feel guilt or anxiety every time you receive or spend.
- You undercharge or overdeliver, then resent it.
- You chase external success but never feel safe or satisfied.
- You avoid financial conversations or hide from your numbers.

These are not moral failings. They are signals. They tell you: *There is an emotion here that wants to move.* When you ignore the signal, the pattern repeats. When you honor it, you break the cycle.

Learning to feel your feelings is not indulgent. It's one of the most potent prosperity practices there is.

How to Transmute Fear into Flow

Transmutation is the process of changing the form or nature of something. In energetic work, it means converting one frequency into another—without denying the original energy. Transmuting fear doesn't mean making it disappear. It means *meeting it fully, moving it through your body, and choosing what comes next.*

Here is a process you can use anytime fear, scarcity, or emotional contraction shows up:

Name It: The first step is awareness. Don't resist the fear. Acknowledge it. Give it a name. Say to yourself: "I feel fear," or "I feel constriction in my chest," or "Something in me feels unsafe right now." Naming separates you from the emotion and creates space.

Locate It: Where is the fear living in your body? Is it in your throat, your gut, your shoulders, your jaw? Bring your awareness there. Don't try to fix it. Just observe. Breathe into it.

Validate It: Speak to the part of you that feels afraid. Use compassionate language: "I see you. You're trying to protect me. You're not wrong for being here." Most fear softens when it feels seen.

Move It: Fear is energy. To transmute it, it must move. Let your body move. Shake. Dance. Sigh loudly. Cry if needed. Stretch. Tap your chest. Even five minutes of physical movement can shift everything.

Ask It: Once the emotion has softened, ask it: "What are you here to teach me?" Sometimes fear carries wisdom—like a need for boundaries, rest, or clarity. Listen without judgment.

Choose Again: Now that the fear has moved, choose a new state. Place your hand on your heart and ask: "What would love/trust/abundance choose right now?" Let that become your next action.

This process takes less time than scrolling your phone—and it's infinitely more transformative.

You don't have to eliminate fear to succeed. You just have to stop letting it drive.

Making Emotion Your Ally

What if every emotion—yes, even the hard ones—was an invitation into greater flow?

Most people categorize emotions as "positive" or "negative," but in energetic terms, all emotion is *information*. Joy and grief, rage and peace—they are all valid. They all carry messages. They all carry power.

Anger, for example, is often seen as destructive. But when honored and channeled, it becomes *clarity*. It tells you what's out of alignment. It gives you the fire to say no, to set boundaries, to stop playing small.

Grief, too, holds profound wisdom. It teaches release. It clears space. It reminds you that you are alive.

Even envy can be a teacher. It reveals desire. It points to what you secretly believe is unavailable—and invites you to make it available.

The more you learn to feel your feelings *without story, without shame*, the more fluid your energy becomes. And fluid energy is magnetic. Prosperity flows to people who are *emotionally available* to receive it.

Start making time each day to check in with your emotional body. Not to judge it. To listen. To feel. To move. To integrate.

This is the opposite of bypassing. This is embodiment. And embodiment is the gateway to everything you want.

The Emotional Vibration of Wealth

Want to know what wealth actually feels like?

It feels like *safety*. Like *relaxation*. Like *peace in your body*. It feels like the absence of urgency and the presence of trust.

When you're emotionally aligned with wealth, you don't rush. You don't grip. You don't prove. You allow. You choose. You create. You receive.

So if you want to raise your financial ceiling, start by regulating your emotional baseline. Shift from fear to trust. From urgency to patience. From proving to knowing.

Here's the secret: emotional mastery is not about controlling how you feel. It's about building the capacity to *stay present* with whatever arises, and then respond from truth—not trauma.

The more emotional capacity you develop, the more prosperity you can hold.

Because real wealth is not just about money. It's about your *ability to be with more*. More love. More responsibility. More joy. More risk. More visibility. More power.

And that ability is forged in the fire of emotional fluency.

You Are a Channel, Not a Container

Emotions are not meant to be stored. They are meant to move. You are not a vault—you are a vessel.

When you let your feelings flow through you, instead of bottling or bypassing them, you become a clear channel. Energy moves. Intuition sharpens. Creativity returns. Abundance flows.

You are not too much. You are not too sensitive. You are not broken for feeling deeply.

Your emotional body is a gift. It is your tuning fork. It is your compass. It is your superpower.

Use it.

PART III: PLAYING BY THE REAL RULES

Chapter 9: The Law of Circulation – Why Hoarding Blocks Wealth

We've been taught to view wealth as something we must acquire and protect, as though it were a finite resource that could vanish at any moment. We are told to save, stockpile, and preserve. While there is value in financial wisdom and planning, the deeper truth is this: **money stagnates when it's hoarded, and it multiplies when it's moved**.

The universe operates on circulation. Rivers flow, seasons turn, breath comes in and goes out. Nothing in nature thrives by withholding. And yet, we often try to create security through accumulation rather than alignment.

Wealth doesn't want to be imprisoned. It wants to circulate through your life, to touch others, to serve, to expand—and to return with interest.

Understanding and embodying the Law of Circulation isn't about reckless spending. It's about releasing contraction. It's about entering into the sacred rhythm of giving and receiving, of letting go and welcoming more, of trusting the current of life.

Hoarding Is a Symptom of Scarcity

Let's be honest: most people hoard not because they're greedy, but because they're afraid. They fear running out. They fear being irresponsible. They fear not being able to replace what they release. This fear creates a survival-based approach to money and energy—one that prioritizes safety over expansion, control over trust.

This mindset is deeply ingrained. It's rooted in generational trauma, economic conditioning, and cultural myths about success and security. We're praised for saving, admired for self-sacrifice, and warned not to be "too generous." As a result, we often equate hoarding with wisdom—even when it's rooted in anxiety.

But here's the energetic truth: **what you hold onto out of fear becomes stagnant, heavy, and limiting**. It doesn't grow. It doesn't inspire. It doesn't breathe.

And this applies far beyond money. Hoarding can look like:
- Holding onto old clothes, ideas, or relationships out of guilt.
- Saving time or energy "just in case" but never investing in joy.
- Withholding compliments, help, or emotional generosity.
- Refusing to spend money on things that would expand your capacity.

All of these behaviors keep you in a pattern of contraction. They send the message: "I don't trust the flow."

That message is powerful. And because energy responds to belief, the more you operate from that message, the more you experience the very lack you're trying to avoid.

To break this cycle, you must make a bold decision: to trust circulation more than stagnation.

Aligned Giving and Conscious Spending

The Law of Circulation doesn't ask you to throw money to the wind. It asks you to **engage with money and resources from a place of trust, intention, and generosity**.

Aligned giving means giving without attachment. It means releasing money, time, energy, or resources without fear, expectation, or martyrdom. It's not about overextending yourself or proving your worth through sacrifice. It's about participating in the flow.

Conscious spending works the same way. Every time you spend from a place of self-love, empowerment, or service, you activate circulation. Every time you invest in your joy, growth, healing, or vision, you signal to the universe: *I am a trustworthy steward of prosperity*.

You can ask yourself before giving or spending:
- Am I doing this from fear or from expansion?
- Is this action aligned with my values and goals?

- Does this support circulation—or contract me further?

When your answer comes from a place of clarity and calm, you're in the flow. When it comes from guilt, scarcity, or a need to prove something, pause and realign.

Examples of high-frequency circulation include:
- Paying someone generously for their time or art.
- Donating to causes that light you up.
- Hiring support that frees you to focus on your purpose.
- Spending money on experiences that energize you.
- Tithing, not to earn favor, but to participate in a sacred exchange.

These actions are not just transactions. They are energetic statements. They declare: *I live in abundance. I trust that more is always available. I am not afraid to let go.*

And what you give from that state—whether it's $10 or $10,000—always returns multiplied, often in surprising and unexpected ways.

Receiving Is Part of the Circulation Cycle

Many people struggle with the Law of Circulation not because they can't give—but because they can't receive.

They've been taught to value self-reliance over interdependence. They fear being a burden. They believe that needing help, accepting gifts, or charging fairly makes them selfish or weak.

But here's the truth: **circulation requires both sides of the current**. You can't be a great giver if you're a poor receiver. When you block receiving, you break the cycle. You become a dam in the flow.

Receiving isn't passive. It's an active, powerful choice. It means saying yes to support, compensation, love, attention, and resources. It means believing that you are worthy—not because you've done enough, but because you *exist*.

To strengthen your receiving muscle, practice:
- Saying "thank you" without deflection when given a compliment or gift.

- Allowing others to help, support, or provide—even when you could do it alone.
- Raising your prices or asking for more with confidence.
- Letting money flow in through unexpected sources without guilt.

As you open to receive, you expand the field. You inspire others to give. You keep the energy moving. You say to the universe: *Yes, I am available for more.*

The More You Give, the More You Become

The Law of Circulation doesn't just make you richer—it makes you *more*. More open. More alive. More connected. More impactful. More aligned with your true essence.

When you give from overflow—not from lack—you activate the deepest truth of prosperity: *You are not the source. You are the channel.*

You don't have to hoard water if you live next to a river. You don't need to grip what you know will be replenished. The more you trust the source—the divine, life, the quantum field—the more you realize you're not losing anything by giving. You're becoming a bigger vessel for it all.

You are not meant to clutch, hide, or shrink. You are meant to circulate, expand, and overflow.

Let that become your new wealth strategy.

Chapter 10: The Law of Expansion – Why Stretching Attracts More

Every living thing is designed to grow. Trees reach for the sky, rivers carve deeper paths, galaxies spin outward. Nature does not contract in fear of failure—it expands because expansion is *what it is*. You, as a human being, are no different. Your spirit craves expansion. Your potential pulls at you, always nudging you toward more expression, more love, more creation, more abundance.

The Law of Expansion is one of the most liberating principles of prosperity. It teaches that abundance responds to *your willingness to stretch beyond the familiar*. That the more you allow yourself to grow—emotionally, mentally, spiritually, financially—the more the universe mirrors that growth with new resources, relationships, and opportunities.

And yet, many of us resist expansion. We confuse comfort with safety. We avoid the unknown. We hold onto what's predictable—even when it no longer serves us—because the idea of stretching feels too risky, too exposed, too unfamiliar.

But the truth is, *prosperity lives beyond your comfort zone*. Not because suffering is required, but because your next level always asks you to become more of who you truly are. It invites you into alignment with your *larger self*—the version of you who is no longer ruled by fear, but by vision.

The question is not whether you're capable of expanding. You are. The question is: *Are you willing to say yes to it—even when it stretches you?*

Why Comfort Zones Become Cages

Your comfort zone is the emotional and energetic territory where you feel most safe. It's the set of circumstances, patterns, and behaviors that feel familiar—regardless of whether they serve you. In fact, many comfort zones are built on scarcity, struggle, or over-responsibility, simply because that's what your system has learned to normalize.

Comfort zones can sound like:
- "This is just how I've always done it."
- "I can't risk that right now."
- "It's not the right time."
- "I'm not ready."
- "I'm afraid of what people will think."

What's important to understand is that your nervous system prefers *familiar pain* over *unfamiliar possibility*. So if success, ease, or visibility feel unfamiliar—even if you consciously want them—your system may resist. It might self-sabotage. It might procrastinate. It might create drama or distractions to bring you back to the known.

This isn't weakness. It's wiring.

But wiring can be changed. The moment you notice the edge of your comfort zone—the moment you feel the fear, resistance, or contraction—you've reached the gateway of expansion. That's where the magic happens. That's where growth begins.

Expanding doesn't mean jumping off a cliff. It means taking *one aligned step beyond the edge* of your usual habits and identity. And then another. And another. Until what once scared you becomes your new normal.

This is how you evolve your capacity. This is how you become someone who can hold, circulate, and attract more.

Stretching Is the Currency of Abundance

Abundance doesn't just respond to desire—it responds to *alignment*. And alignment means becoming someone who is willing to stretch.

You may desire a thriving business, a larger income, or a platform for your voice. But are you willing to stretch into visibility, leadership, responsibility, or rejection? That's the real question.

Stretching doesn't mean forcing. It doesn't mean performing or proving. It means *expanding your container*—your inner framework for what you believe is possible, sustainable, and safe.

When you stretch, you communicate to the universe: "I trust myself with more."

And in response, more becomes available.

Stretching can look like:
- Charging more for your work, even if it feels scary.
- Saying yes to an opportunity that feels slightly out of reach.
- Setting a boundary you've always avoided.
- Investing in yourself, your business, or your healing.
- Speaking your truth when your voice is shaking.
- Doing the thing before you feel "ready."

These actions don't have to be grand. They just have to be *true*. Each one sends a signal that you are no longer ruled by the identity of limitation.

Stretching is not about discomfort for its own sake. It's about *becoming a vibrational match for the life you're calling in*.

And here's the paradox: while stretching can feel scary, the result is often *greater ease*. Because living out of alignment—shrinking, hiding, settling—is actually exhausting. Expansion, while confronting, brings energy, clarity, and joy.

Your body knows this. Every time you stretch, you feel more alive.

From Expansion Anxiety to Expansion Mastery

So how do you stretch when it feels terrifying? How do you say yes to growth when your mind is screaming, "Not yet"?

The answer lies in developing *expansion resilience*—the emotional and nervous system capacity to stay present during transformation.

Here are powerful ways to build that resilience:

Normalize Discomfort

Discomfort doesn't mean you're doing it wrong. It means you're doing something *new*. When you expect some resistance, you stop fearing it. You realize it's just your system calibrating to a higher level.

Move in Micro-Stretches

You don't have to overhaul your life. Choose tiny expansions. If you normally charge $100, try $125. If you usually avoid networking, reach out to one new person. Small stretches build trust and momentum.

Use Somatic Anchoring

When you're stretching, keep your body engaged. Breathe deeply. Ground your feet. Tap your chest. Speak out loud. Movement helps your system process intensity without collapsing.

Celebrate Immediately

Every time you stretch—even if the result is messy—celebrate the fact that you did it. Praise rewires your brain. It teaches your system that expansion is rewarding.

Surround Yourself with Expanders

Spend time with people who are living at the level you're stepping into. Their nervous systems will help co-regulate yours. You'll see that it's possible, and more importantly, *safe*.

Rest After Growth Spurts

Expansion is work. It taxes your emotional system. After big stretches, give yourself recovery time. Naps, nature, quiet, or journaling help integrate the shift.

The more you stretch, the less dramatic it becomes. What once triggered fear becomes normal. Your ceiling becomes your floor. And then you stretch again.

This is how expansion becomes a lifestyle—not a one-time event.

You Are Meant to Grow

The Law of Expansion reminds you of a fundamental truth: **you are not here to stay small**. You are not here to repeat patterns, suppress your gifts, or shrink your vision to make others comfortable.

You are here to *become*—to unfold, to express, to create, to stretch. Prosperity is not a static goal. It is a living process. And your job is to keep saying yes to that process, even when it feels uncertain.

Your income, impact, joy, and flow will always rise to meet the level of expansion you're willing to embody.
So stretch.
Speak louder than before. Stand taller. Ask for more. Receive more. Circulate more. Trust more.
You will not break. You will grow.
And with every expansion, you make space for more abundance—not just for you, but for everyone your life touches.

Chapter 11: The Law of Embodiment – Be Before You Have

Most people live by a conditional formula: *Once I have the money, the time, the confidence—then I'll be who I want to be.* Once the external reality changes, then I'll allow myself to feel different. More worthy. More powerful. More joyful.

But real transformation flips that logic. According to the Law of Embodiment, you must *be* the person first. You must step into the identity, energy, and posture of your future self *before* the circumstances arrive. This is not delusion—it's creation.

You do not attract what you want. You attract what you *are*. Your reality reflects your identity, not your wish list. And this is where most people stay stuck. They wait for their life to change so they can feel abundant, powerful, or free. But the Law of Embodiment says: *Feel those things now—and life will align around you.*

Who Are You Willing to Be?

Every morning you wake up with a choice: to continue living as the version of you shaped by the past, or to step into the version of you shaped by your vision. That choice determines the energy you carry, the decisions you make, and the opportunities you magnetize.

Embodiment begins with that decision.

The first step is to identify the embodied version of you who already lives in your desired reality. This is not fantasy—it's a higher aspect of you that already exists in potential. Your job is to connect with them, study them, and begin living *as them*.

Start by asking yourself:
- What does the prosperous version of me believe about money, worth, and flow?
- How do they carry themselves?
- How do they treat their body, time, and boundaries?
- What do they no longer tolerate?
- What are their daily rituals, habits, and priorities?

- How do they speak to themselves in private?
- What decisions do they make without overthinking?

This is not about pretending. It's about tuning into a frequency that's already within you, but hasn't yet been consistently expressed. That version of you is already coded in your field. You just haven't made it your dominant state—yet.

Choose one or two qualities from your future self and begin practicing them now. Start small. Embodiment happens through repetition, not performance. Walk like her. Speak like him. Think like them. Dress, invest, move, and create from that identity.

Every time you do, you reinforce the signal: *I am already her. I already live there. This is who I am now.* That signal is powerful. It bends reality.

Action From Identity, Not Insecurity

Most people take action from insecurity. They do things to prove their worth, avoid judgment, or chase validation. This creates misaligned energy—an undercurrent of fear that taints every effort. Even when results come, they feel hollow or temporary.

Embodiment asks you to take action from a different place: from *identity*. From the knowing that you already are enough. Already capable. Already worthy of receiving.

This is the difference between efforting and alignment. When you take action as the person who already trusts themselves, you stop forcing. You stop chasing. You stop second-guessing every move. Your energy stabilizes, and your results become more consistent.

Let's say you're launching a new offer or applying for a new job. You could take action from fear: "What if they don't buy? What if I'm not ready? What if I fail?" Or you could take action from embodiment: "This is who I am. I trust the right people will feel it. I'm building momentum, not seeking validation."

Same task. Totally different vibration. And because your outer results are shaped by your inner state, the outcomes will reflect that.

Living the Frequency Now

The final piece of embodiment is emotional. It's not enough to intellectually align with your future self—you must *feel* them in your body. Embodiment is vibrational. You must carry the frequency now, not wait for permission.

If your desired life feels light, free, grounded, and expansive—practice those feelings now. Generate them. Anchor them. Let your nervous system get familiar with what you've been waiting for.

Don't wait for the money to feel wealthy. Don't wait for the partner to feel loved. Don't wait for the promotion to feel powerful. Those feelings are a frequency you can access *right now*. They're already in you. Your job is to stabilize them.

How?

- **Visualization with emotion**: Close your eyes. See your future self. Let it be vivid. But most importantly, *feel* how they feel. Let that energy fill your cells.
- **Daily embodiment rituals**: Wake up and ask, "What does the version of me who already has it all do today?" Then do one small thing that matches that frequency.
- **Somatic anchoring**: When you feel powerful, place your hand on your heart or belly. Breathe. Say, "This is what power feels like. This is mine." The body remembers.
- **Declutter misaligned energy**: Notice when you're operating from your old self—complaining, shrinking, doubting. Pause. Shift. Embody again.

Embodiment is not about perfection. It's about repetition. Frequency responds to consistency, not drama. Be the person, every day, in the smallest ways you can.

Over time, you'll look around and realize: *I'm living in what I used to visualize*. Not because you forced it. But because you became it.

Your Identity Shapes Your Reality

At its core, the Law of Embodiment is about identity. Who you believe yourself to be is the foundation of what you allow yourself to receive.

When you shift your identity from the inside out, your outer world cannot help but change. Opportunities align. People respond differently. Money flows more easily. And most importantly, you feel at home in your own skin.

This is how lasting wealth is built—not just in numbers, but in *being*. You stop performing prosperity. You start living it.

You don't wait for success to prove who you are. You live from who you are, and success becomes inevitable.

You don't wait to be chosen. You realize you were the one choosing all along.

Chapter 12: The Law of Resonance – Match What You Want

Many people believe that desire alone is enough to create change. They make vision boards, write affirmations, and set intentions—but still feel stuck. The truth is, the universe doesn't respond to what you *want*. It responds to what you *resonate* with.

Resonance is the energetic frequency you emit—your baseline vibration. It's not determined by the positive thoughts you think once in a while, but by the feelings, beliefs, and identities you embody consistently. It's what you truly expect, deep down. What you assume to be possible, available, and normal for you.

The Law of Resonance teaches us that life reflects back to us the energy we hold most often. If you vibrate in scarcity, even if you long for wealth, you'll attract circumstances that mirror lack. If you vibrate in trust, opportunities begin to align. Resonance is a mirror, not a wish-granting machine.

This chapter is about learning how to calibrate your frequency to match what you desire—not by faking or forcing, but by becoming energetically coherent. Because when your internal signal aligns with your desired external reality, reality shifts to match.

The Resonance You Don't Know You're Broadcasting

Every moment of your life, you're broadcasting a frequency. Not with your words alone, but with your posture, your thoughts, your self-talk, your emotions, and your energy. Most of this is unconscious. It's shaped by your history, your habits, your nervous system, and your identity.

Imagine walking into a room and meeting someone who says, "Everything is great!" but their body is tense, their eyes dart around, and their voice quivers. You can *feel* that they're not being congruent. Their energy is saying something different than their words. That's resonance at work.

In the same way, you may say, "I want to be wealthy," but if your inner vibration is broadcasting fear, guilt, or shame around money, the universe responds to *that*, not your statement. This is not punishment—it's energetic feedback. And it's actually a gift.

When you start to take responsibility for the resonance you're emitting, you reclaim your power. You stop waiting for things to change and begin working with the laws of energy consciously. Start by asking:

- What emotional state do I live in most of the time?
- What beliefs do I rehearse in my head?
- How does my body respond to the idea of having what I want?
- Do I trust life—or brace against it?
- What's the dominant vibration of my thoughts about money, love, and success?

These questions help you become aware of your true signal—not what you want to project, but what you actually are projecting. Awareness is always the first step toward recalibration.

Coherence: Aligning Thoughts, Feelings, and Behavior

Resonance is not about a single element—it's about coherence. Coherence is when your thoughts, feelings, and actions are all aligned and reinforcing the same signal.

If you think positively but feel unworthy, there's static in your signal. If you affirm wealth but act from fear, you dilute your resonance. But when all parts of you agree—when your thoughts affirm possibility, your feelings rest in trust, and your actions reflect belief—you become magnetic.

This is why embodiment, as discussed in the previous chapter, is so powerful. Embodiment creates coherence. It brings your energy into agreement. You no longer say one thing and feel another. You *are* what you seek. That's when the universe listens.

Creating coherence is a practice. It requires choosing congruence over contradiction. For example:

- If you say you trust the process, but obsessively check your bank account, that's contradiction.
- If you say you want more time, but overbook yourself, that's contradiction.
- If you say you want expansion, but only take action from fear, that's contradiction.

To recalibrate, start small. Ask yourself daily: *What would full coherence look like today?* Maybe it's one decision made from peace. One email sent with confidence. One moment of genuine gratitude.

Over time, these small alignments shift your baseline resonance. You start to embody trust more than doubt. Gratitude more than grasping. And those frequencies become the magnets that reshape your life.

Becoming a Resonant Match for Your Next Level

Once you understand the mechanics of resonance, the question becomes: *What do I need to become in order to attract what I desire?* Not in a performative sense, but energetically.

This is where the practice of *tuning* comes in. Just as a musician tunes their instrument to the key of a song, you can tune your energy to the frequency of your next level. You do this through emotion, attention, and action.

Let's break this down.

Emotional Tuning

Every goal has an emotional signature. Wealth might feel like freedom. Love might feel like safety. Success might feel like confidence. Begin practicing those emotions *now*, even before the outcome arrives. This isn't faking—it's *practicing the frequency*.

Close your eyes. Feel into the desired version of your life. What does it feel like in your body? Warmth? Openness? Groundedness? Let that become your new baseline.

Attention Tuning

What you focus on expands. If your attention is constantly on problems, lack, or fear, your resonance stays low. Train your attention on gratitude, vision, and solutions. Read books, listen to content, and consume stories that affirm the frequency you want to live in.

Curate your environment as if your frequency depends on it—because it does.

Behavioral Tuning

Act like the version of you who already trusts. Make the investment, raise the boundary, decline the misaligned offer. Even small acts of alignment shift your resonance. Every behavior says something energetically: "This is who I am. This is what I expect."

Tuning is not about being high-vibe all the time. It's about coming back to alignment over and over again. Your power is not in perfection—it's in recalibration.

As your resonance rises, you'll notice subtle shifts. People treat you differently. Ideas flow more easily. Resources appear. What once felt out of reach begins to feel inevitable. This is not magic. It's resonance.

Your Frequency Is Your Invitation

Ultimately, the Law of Resonance reminds you that your life is not happening *to* you—it's happening *through* you.

You are constantly sending invitations through your vibration. The question is: what are you inviting in?

If you want different results, you must become a different signal. Not louder, not needier—just clearer. Cleaner. More aligned.

This is why inner work is not optional. You can't fake resonance. You can't affirm your way into coherence if you're ignoring the fear beneath it. But when you commit to feeling, healing, and choosing again, you begin to tune your energy like a master.

You stop begging for your desires—and start *matching* them.

Resonance is not about striving. It's about returning. Returning to your truth. Returning to your power. Returning to the part of you that already knows how to create.

PART IV: PRACTICAL PROSPERITY

Chapter 13: The $0 to Wealth Shift Plan

There's a moment on every prosperity journey when you look around and realize you're not starting from abundance—you're starting from survival. Maybe your bank account is empty. Maybe you're in debt. Maybe you're earning, but it's never enough. Or maybe you've plateaued, stuck in a loop that feels impossible to break.

This chapter is for that moment. It's for when you feel like you're starting from zero—or less than zero. It's when all the talk about alignment, vibration, and energy feels distant, like a theory that applies to other people but not you.

And yet, this is where true wealth-building begins.

Not when you have the funds, the business, the support, or the confidence—but when you decide to shift your state despite appearances. The $0 to Wealth Shift Plan isn't about quick money. It's about building the foundation of a new reality—one where wealth becomes inevitable because *you* have changed.

No matter how little you have right now, you have everything you need to begin this shift. You have agency. You have presence. You have the ability to choose a new frequency today—and to take consistent, grounded actions from that frequency. That's how the current turns.

Let's begin with the very first step: mastering your inner economy.

Step 1: Mastering Your Internal State

Your outer world will never sustainably outperform your inner world. That's why the first shift has nothing to do with money and everything to do with energy. You must decide—right now—that your value is not determined by your balance sheet.

You are not your overdraft. You are not your credit score. You are not the zeros in your account. You are the field in which money flows, and you can upgrade that field starting today.

The inner shift begins with awareness. Ask yourself:
- What story am I telling myself about my current financial situation?
- Am I narrating lack, shame, blame, or powerlessness?
- What would change if I shifted my story to one of reclamation?

Instead of saying, "I'm broke," try: "I'm building."
Instead of, "I don't have enough," try: "I'm opening to receive."
Instead of, "I messed everything up," try: "I'm learning how to create differently."
This isn't toxic positivity. It's energetic reorientation. You're not denying your circumstances—you're refusing to identify with them.
Every morning, before you check your phone or email, tune into the wealth that already exists: breath, sun, safety, choice, creativity. Anchor in gratitude, not to manipulate the universe, but to regulate your nervous system. When you feel safe, you access new ideas. When you feel worthy, you move differently. This is step one.
Add to that a five-minute daily embodiment practice. Stand in front of the mirror, breathe deeply, and affirm who you are becoming:
- "I am open to wealth in all forms."
- "I trust money to flow to me and through me."
- "I take powerful action every day, even in small ways."

Over time, this internal state becomes your new default. From there, you begin to act—and this is where shift becomes strategy.

Step 2: Create Micro-Momentum with Aligned Action

When you're starting from zero, the path forward can feel overwhelming. That's why the second step of the $0 to Wealth Shift Plan is to *generate micro-momentum*. These are small, strategic actions that move you from passive to active energy—from waiting to creating.

Here's how to build micro-momentum:

Clean Up Leaks

What subscriptions, habits, or patterns are silently draining your energy and finances? Cancel what's not aligned. Say no where you've been over-giving. Create space.

Monetize Your Skills (Without Overthinking)
You don't need to build a six-figure brand overnight. You just need to offer something of value. Can you edit, write, coach, teach, organize, support, fix, design, or listen? Offer it. Tell your community. Post on social media. Reach out to five people. Focus on service, not perfection.

Sell What You Already Have
Look around. Books, clothes, gadgets, tools. There is probably $50 to $500 worth of forgotten abundance in your home. Decluttering creates circulation and sends a signal: *I'm willing to move energy.*

Set a 30-Day Prosperity Challenge
Every day for the next 30 days, do one thing that supports your financial expansion. Make an ask. Pitch yourself. Update your profile. Apply for something. Follow up. Show up. One thing a day = 30 new waves of energy.

Create a Money Activation Jar
This may sound playful, but it's powerful. Label a jar "Money I Called In." Every time money comes in—even if it's $1—put a note in the jar. At the end of 30 days, you'll see physical evidence of your magnetism. This builds confidence and momentum.

These actions are not about hustling. They're about becoming someone who moves from belief, not fear. When you combine internal alignment with consistent outer action, you begin to shift both your vibration and your results.

Step 3: Build a New Relationship With Wealth

The final piece of this shift is relational. Money is not just currency—it's a relationship. And just like any relationship, it responds to how you treat it.

If you ignore money, resent it, fear it, or chase it desperately, it doesn't feel safe in your space. But when you nurture it, respect it, and allow it to flow, it feels welcome. That's when it stays. That's when it grows.

Here's how to build a healthier relationship with money:

Meet With Your Money Weekly

Even if you don't have much yet, sit down once a week and review your finances. Track what came in. Track what went out. Celebrate any win—no matter how small. Light a candle. Make it sacred.

Stop Shaming Your Spending

When you spend, do it from choice—not guilt. Ask yourself: *Does this reflect who I want to become?* If yes, bless the purchase. If not, shift it next time. Either way, release shame.

Start a Wealth Practice

Set aside time every week to read about money, visualize wealth, organize your finances, or plan your next move. Treat it like you would any sacred ritual. This builds emotional safety and energetic clarity.

Talk About Money With Empowered People

Scarcity thrives in silence. Start having real conversations with friends, mentors, or communities where wealth is normalized. Exposure rewires you. When you hear people discuss money without fear, you internalize that safety.

Ask Your Money What It Wants

This may sound strange, but ask: *Money, what do you want me to know?* Then listen. You might be surprised by the insights that arise. Money is not just paper. It's energy. And it has a message for you.

The more you build intimacy with money, the less intimidating it becomes. It stops being a mystery or monster. It becomes a companion in your expansion.

From this place, you're no longer trying to escape zero—you're laying a foundation for overflow.

You're Already In Motion

The $0 to Wealth Shift Plan is not a miracle pill. It's a method for energetic re-alignment, practical action, and identity evolution. It honors your current reality while activating your future one.

You don't have to leap. You just have to shift—daily, gently, powerfully.

Start where you are. Move what you can. Tune your energy. Take aligned action. Tend to your relationship with money.

And most of all, remember: wealth doesn't begin with dollars. It begins with decisions. The decision to no longer abandon yourself. The decision to believe, even when the numbers say otherwise. The decision to build a new story—one action, one breath, one aligned moment at a time.

Chapter 14: Money Management for Energy-Smart People

When you begin to receive more money—whether through a job, a business, or unexpected channels—the next test is not how to earn, but how to manage. Money management is not just about budgeting or investing. It's about alignment. It's about how you hold, circulate, and relate to money *without shrinking your soul*.

Most people who start earning more fall into one of two traps: either they hoard it out of fear or spend it chaotically because they've never felt safe with it. Both come from the same root issue—an unhealed relationship with money.

If money is a mirror, then your financial habits are energetic feedback. Are you grounded or reactive? Empowered or avoidant? Trusting or defensive?

Energy-smart money management isn't about spreadsheets and calculators—although those tools can help. It's about creating a system that reflects your values, supports your nervous system, and *amplifies your capacity to receive and hold more*.

Managing money consciously means money feels safe in your field. And when money feels safe with you, it stays, grows, and returns with friends.

Let's begin by redefining your emotional framework around money—so that the numbers can align with the new energy you're carrying.

Releasing Shame and Rebuilding Safety

Before you can manage money well, you must first feel *safe* with money. And for most people, that safety has been fractured by years of scarcity, judgment, or inherited patterns.

Shame is the most common block to effective money management. It whispers, "You should be further along by now." It says, "You're bad with money." It keeps you from looking at your bank account, opening your statements, or asking for help.

The first step to becoming energy-smart with money is to *release the shame* and normalize your current financial reality—not as a reflection of your worth, but as a snapshot in time. Money is data, not identity. You are not your debt. You are not your spending history. You are not behind. You're just now becoming aware—and that awareness is a portal to new wealth.

Here are practices to help you rebuild safety:

1. **Create a Safe Space for Money Conversations**
   Instead of tackling your finances in a rush or under stress, choose a calm moment each week—light a candle, play music, pour tea. Make it a ritual. The more relaxed your body is, the more honest and clear your mind will be.
2. **Write a Money Forgiveness Letter**
   Write a letter from your higher self to your past self. Acknowledge the ways you've mishandled money—and offer compassion, not punishment. Say: "You did the best you could with what you knew. And now, we begin again."
3. **Stop Using Money as a Moral Scorecard**
   You are not more evolved if you save or less spiritual if you spend. Money is neutral. It becomes meaningful based on the intention and energy behind it. Detach your identity from your numbers.

When you clear shame, you can finally see money for what it is: a tool, a resource, a flow. And then, you're ready to structure it with consciousness.

Building a System That Honors Your Energy

The point of managing your money is not control—it's *clarity*. When you know what's coming in, what's going out, and where it's going, you feel more powerful, not more limited. You stop avoiding and start *choosing*.

Let's build a simple, soul-aligned system that you can use—whether you're making $500 a month or $50,000.

Give Every Dollar a Job

This is the golden rule of money management. Unassigned money disappears quickly. Assigned money grows. As soon as money enters your life, *tell it where to go* based on your priorities.

Use these basic energetic buckets:
- **Essentials (50%)**: Rent, bills, groceries—what you need to stay grounded.
- **Expansion (20%)**: Education, healing, support, coaching, business tools—anything that helps you grow.
- **Overflow (10%)**: Savings, investments, emergency fund—money that builds long-term security.
- **Circulation (10%)**: Giving, donating, tipping, blessing others—money that keeps energy moving.
- **Joy + Desire (10%)**: Fun, travel, beauty, art—money that signals you're safe to enjoy wealth now.

These percentages aren't rigid—they're a starting point. Adjust them based on your life, but ensure each bucket is honored. Especially the ones most neglected.

Automate What You Can

Automation is energetic trust in action. It says, "I trust that money will keep flowing, so I'm setting up systems that reflect that." Automate your savings, bill payments, and recurring investments. Take the pressure off your nervous system to remember and control everything.

Use a Sacred Money Tracker

Track every dollar that enters your life—not to obsess, but to *celebrate*. Create a Google Sheet, use an app, or write it in a journal. When money comes in, write down the amount, the source, and how it made you feel. Over time, you'll see patterns. You'll also build gratitude and awareness.

Check In Weekly

Money avoidance breeds chaos. Wealth consciousness requires visibility. Every week, have a 15-minute check-in: What came in? What went out? What needs adjustment? What am I proud of?

When you treat your money like a living, breathing relationship, it thrives.

Expanding Your Capacity to Hold More

One of the most underrated parts of wealth-building is learning how to *hold* money. Not just receive it—but hold it with confidence, without fear, and without immediately needing to spend, prove, or offload it.

This is nervous system work.

If you've been in survival mode for a long time, receiving more money can actually feel unsafe. You may unconsciously repel it, overspend it, or sabotage your success—not because you're foolish, but because your system doesn't yet feel at home with abundance.

Here's how to expand your holding capacity:

1. **Practice Holding $100 Without Spending It**
   This simple exercise rewires your sense of safety. Take $100 (or whatever amount stretches you slightly), place it in your wallet, and carry it without touching it. Feel the power of having money you *don't need to use*. Let it remind you that you are not in lack.

2. **Breathe When You Look at Your Bank Account**
   Before you open your banking app, pause. Take five deep breaths. Regulate your body. Look at the number with neutrality. Say: "This is just where I'm starting today." Stay present. This builds capacity.

3. **Visualize Yourself Holding Wealth Calmly**
   Close your eyes and imagine large sums of money entering your account. Watch yourself smile, stay grounded, feel safe. Do this often. Teach your body that having more is safe, even boring.

4. **Detach from Sudden Outcomes**
   Not every month will be exponential. But every aligned month builds trust. Don't measure your worth by

fluctuations. Measure it by how consistently you honor your system.

Wealth doesn't just grow from income. It grows from *integration*. And when your nervous system feels safe with more, more becomes sustainable.

Be the Steward, Not the Servant

Ultimately, managing money as an energy-smart person is about becoming a *steward*, not a servant. You are not a slave to your bills. You are not a victim of your patterns. You are the creator of your flow.

Stewardship means you don't just count money—you *bless* it. You direct it with purpose. You use it to build a life that nourishes your soul, not drains it.

Money doesn't demand perfection. It asks for partnership. When you show up consistently, cleanly, and consciously—it shows up for you.

Chapter 15: The Prosperity Rituals That Actually Work

There is a profound difference between random effort and ritualized intention. One is scattered energy that burns out quickly. The other is sacred structure that builds momentum. Prosperity, contrary to what we're often taught, doesn't just arrive through strategy—it flows through rhythm.

When your days are chaotic, when your habits are reactive, and when your energy is fragmented, you cut yourself off from flow. But when you bring rhythm into your life—when you show up consistently for your energy, your goals, and your wealth field—you begin to stabilize abundance.

Rituals are not about superstition. They're about energetic repetition. They tell your system: "This is who I am. This is what we do. This is what we're available for." Over time, rituals sculpt your identity. They carve out a version of you who is grounded, focused, and in harmony with prosperity.

This chapter is about the rituals that actually shift things—not fluff, not hustle—but real practices that open your field, regulate your nervous system, and align your actions with your desires.

You don't need 50 rituals. You need a few that you do with presence, devotion, and consistency. These are the ones that work.

Morning Rituals: Activating the Field

The first moments of your day are the most powerful. They determine your emotional baseline and energetic signal. If you wake up and immediately check your phone, absorb other people's stress, and rush into reaction—you start the day in contraction.

But if you wake up and center yourself first, you activate your wealth field. You step into the frequency of leadership, clarity, and receptivity.

Here's a simple morning ritual sequence that takes 15–30 minutes and sets the tone for prosperity:

1. **Wake With Intention**

    Before you even get out of bed, place your hand on your heart and say: "Thank you. I'm alive. I'm here to receive. I'm here to create." This anchors gratitude without bypassing reality. It also signals your body to feel safe.

2. **Move Energy Through Your Body**

    Even five minutes of movement—stretching, breathwork, a short walk—will clear stagnation and open your field. Movement is manifestation. When your body flows, your life flows.

3. **Tune Your Frequency With Words**

    Speak three affirmations that match the version of you you're becoming. Choose ones that feel just stretchy enough to challenge your current identity without triggering resistance. Examples:

    - "I create money with ease and joy."

    - "My energy attracts aligned opportunities."

    - "Wealth is my normal state."

Say them slowly. Feel them in your body. Let them become a vibration, not just words.

4. **Visualize the Day From Prosperity**

    Close your eyes and imagine your day unfolding with clarity, abundance, and trust. See yourself completing tasks with ease, handling money with confidence, receiving surprises with joy. This trains your brain to expect flow.

5. **Ask a Power Question**

    Instead of to-do lists, ask: "What does the most abundant version of me focus on today?" Then choose one thing. This turns your attention from survival to creation.

When you start your day this way—even if just partially—you raise your energetic baseline. You show up differently. You act from center, not from chaos. This is how you build consistency that compounds.

Evening Rituals: Closing the Loop and Expanding Trust

Most people end their day in stress or distraction. They scroll themselves to sleep, worry about tomorrow, or replay everything that went wrong. This keeps your system in contraction overnight. It reinforces anxiety, not prosperity.

A prosperity-focused evening ritual helps you *close the energy loop* of the day and return to trust. It tells your body and mind: "We're safe. We're learning. We're growing. And we're still on track."

Here's a powerful 3-part ritual to end your day with wealth consciousness:

1. **Reflect Without Judgment**

    Ask yourself: What did I do today that aligned with the version of me I'm becoming? Write down three wins. They don't have to be big. Even small choices count. This reinforces progress and builds self-trust.

Then ask: Where did I act from fear or lack? Again, write it down without judgment. Awareness is power. Shame is not required.

2. **Forgive and Release**

    Say out loud: "I forgive myself for anything I didn't do perfectly. I release today with love. I trust that tomorrow is another chance." This clears stuck energy and prevents you from looping on regret.

3. **Gratitude and Pre-Sleep Visioning**

    Before you sleep, list three things you're grateful for—not just for what happened, but for what's coming. Example: "I'm grateful for the clients who are already on their way. I'm grateful for the money I'm learning to receive."

Then spend one minute visualizing yourself waking up in even greater alignment. Feel it. Smile. Let that vibration settle into your subconscious.

Sleep is a bridge. When you end the day in coherence, your system rests, recovers, and reprograms itself in support of your next level.

Weekly and Monthly Rituals: Grounding the Journey

While daily rituals build momentum, weekly and monthly rituals build *structure*. They give you the chance to zoom out, check your progress, recalibrate your energy, and anchor your intentions.

Here are the most effective long-term prosperity rituals you can incorporate:

Weekly Wealth Check-In

Once a week—same day, same time—sit down with your money. Review what came in, what went out, and how you feel about it. This is not about guilt. It's about intimacy.

Ask: What money flowed to me this week? What did I circulate with love? Where can I align more next week?

Light a candle. Make it sacred. Treat it like a date, not a chore.

Energetic Reset Session

Choose one day each week to do a 30-minute energy cleanse. This can include breathwork, a nature walk, journaling, cold showers, or dancing. The goal is to shake off the energy of the world and return to *your field*.

Ask: What am I carrying that isn't mine? What wants to be cleared? What wants to grow?

Monthly Vision Ritual

At the start of each month, take time to dream. Ask:
- What do I desire to receive this month?
- How do I want to feel in my work, body, and finances?
- What beliefs am I choosing to embody?

Write it down. Speak it aloud. Then choose one anchoring action to embody the vision—something small, doable, but meaningful.

This ritual is your monthly alignment checkpoint. It reminds you that you're not just reacting to life—you're designing it.

Rituals Make You Magnetic

The real power of ritual isn't the tasks themselves—it's who you become through them. Rituals make you someone who shows up. Someone who pays attention. Someone who values alignment more than urgency.

When you have rituals, you stop waiting for motivation. You start living by intention. You stop spiraling into doubt. You start anchoring into truth.

The most magnetic people aren't hustling. They're steady. They're grounded. They're in rhythm. Their presence is felt. And that's what rituals do—they shape your presence.

You don't need to do everything perfectly. You just need to begin. Choose one ritual. Practice it daily for a week. Then build from there. Momentum is built in layers.

Chapter 16: From Scarcity to Overflow – The 90-Day Reset

If you're reading this chapter, you likely already know what it feels like to be stuck in scarcity. Not just financial lack—but emotional contraction, mental looping, energetic fatigue. You've tried affirmations, made vision boards, maybe even started budgeting. But despite all your efforts, the results haven't stuck.

That's because changing your relationship with prosperity isn't about setting one big goal. It's about resetting your *foundation*. Not just doing more—but becoming different.

A reset is not a hustle sprint. It's not a challenge to prove your worth. It's a season of strategic realignment. A conscious decision to shift your energy, thoughts, actions, and habits into a new state of receptivity and flow.

The next 90 days can transform your entire reality—not because you grind harder, but because you operate from a different internal blueprint. This chapter is your step-by-step roadmap.

You'll learn how to clear the residue of scarcity, activate prosperity through structured rituals, and rewire your nervous system for overflow. Whether you're starting from rock bottom or already building momentum, this reset will take you deeper.

Let's start with the first 30 days: detoxing scarcity from your field.

Phase 1: Clearing Scarcity (Days 1–30)

Before you can anchor overflow, you have to make space. Scarcity is not just a financial issue—it's an energetic imprint. It lives in your habits, language, environment, and relationships. Phase One is about detoxing those scarcity signals so you stop reinforcing the frequency you want to leave behind.

Here's what to focus on for your first month:

1. **Audit Your Inputs**

    Scarcity thrives on repetition. Look at your media, social feeds, conversations, and thought patterns. Ask: What am

I consuming that keeps me in fear, comparison, or contraction?

Replace daily scrolling with uplifting content. Unfollow accounts that trigger lack. Read or listen to material that expands your beliefs about wealth and possibility.

2. **Shift Your Language**

    Catch and change any language that reinforces limitation. Phrases like "I can't afford that," "That's too expensive," "Money is tight," "I'm broke," or "It's just not possible for me" are energetic contracts.

Replace them with expansive truths, even if they feel stretchy:
- "It's not a priority right now, but I'm opening to more."
- "I'm learning to create resources with ease."
- "I'm expanding into overflow."

Speak life into your future—not just your past.

3. **Simplify and Declutter**

    Clutter is stuck energy. When your space is full of unused, unloved, or chaotic items, your nervous system stays in low-grade alert. Spend the first 30 days decluttering your home, workspace, phone, and digital life.

Each item you release is a signal: *I trust that what I need will come. I am not defined by old versions of myself.*

4. **Money Inventory Ritual**

    One of the bravest and most empowering things you can do is face your financial reality without judgment. Make a list of all your accounts, debts, income streams, recurring bills, and subscriptions. No shame. Just data.

Do this as a sacred ritual. Light a candle. Breathe. Look at the numbers and say: "I see you. I'm choosing something new." You cannot shift what you refuse to see.

5. **Energy Hygiene Practice**

    Each day, take 5–10 minutes to reset your nervous system. This can be breathwork, meditation, walking, or journaling. The goal is to come back into your body. When you are grounded, you stop reacting from survival mode—and start choosing from power.

The goal of Phase One isn't perfection. It's awareness. Begin to notice where scarcity lives in your daily life—and gently release it. As you clear, you'll start to feel more space, more breath, more capacity.

Then you'll be ready to build.

Phase 2: Building Prosperity Habits (Days 31–60)

Now that you've cleared space, it's time to plant the seeds of prosperity. This middle phase is about creating consistent habits that support your new wealth identity. You're moving from theory to embodiment.

Here's what to focus on during this phase:

1. **Daily Prosperity Practice**

   Commit to 15 minutes each morning to anchor your frequency. This can include:
   - Speaking affirmations out loud
   - Journaling "as if" from your wealthy self
   - Visualizing your next level
   - Practicing gratitude not just for what you have—but what you're receiving

This anchors the belief: *I am already in the energy of wealth.*

2. **Prosperity Tracking**

   Every day, track all forms of abundance that come to you—money, gifts, ideas, compliments, insights, synchronicities. Write them in a notebook or app.

You'll start to see how much is already flowing. This rewires your brain to expect and notice wealth, not just chase it.

3. **Aligned Income Action**

   Take one action daily or weekly that builds income. Whether it's posting an offer, applying for a new opportunity, networking, or refining your skills—move energy.

But the key is: do it from alignment, not desperation. Ask, "What would my most prosperous self do today?" Then act from that place.

4. Money Flow Ritual

Create a weekly ritual for reviewing your finances—not just to check what you have, but to celebrate it. Name the money. Bless the money. Direct the money.

When you treat money as a sacred partner, it wants to stay. It wants to grow.

5. Wealth Embodiment Movement

Your body needs to feel the frequency of prosperity. Once a week, do an embodiment practice:

- Dress as your wealthy self and walk with power
- Dance to music that makes you feel abundant
- Move in a way that says "I belong in overflow"

This phase is about consistency, not drama. Prosperity is not a spike—it's a rhythm. Your goal is to live from wealth, not just wish for it.

Phase 3: Expanding Into Overflow (Days 61–90)

By this point, you've cleared scarcity and started building prosperity habits. Now it's time to *expand*. This phase stretches your capacity—your ability to receive more, hold more, and circulate more.

Overflow isn't just about having more money. It's about becoming someone who creates and receives without fear, guilt, or collapse. It's about upgrading your internal ceiling.

Here's how to expand:

1. Stretch With Intention

Choose one area where you're ready to expand. Maybe it's raising your prices, asking for a raise, investing in your growth, or setting stronger financial boundaries.

Make one bold move that your past self wouldn't have dared. Let your nervous system know: *We can do hard things—and thrive.*

2. Upgrade Your Environment

Look around. What in your space still reflects scarcity? Your wardrobe, workspace, tech, or décor?

Make small upgrades—not to impress others, but to signal to yourself: *We live differently now.* A new pen, a cleaner desk, a fresh playlist. Small shifts change energy.

3. **Give From Overflow**

   Generosity is a sign of abundance. Choose one act of giving each week—tip someone, donate, support a friend, gift something.

But do it from joy, not obligation. Give what *feels* good. When you give freely, you reinforce: *There's always more where that came from.*

4. **Host a Prosperity Integration Day**

   Near the end of your 90 days, block off a half-day or evening to reflect and integrate. Journal what's changed. List your wins. Acknowledge your growth.

Ask: Who am I now? What does overflow feel like? What am I available for moving forward?

5. **Create Your Overflow Identity Statement**

   Write a declaration of who you are now. Include beliefs, behaviors, boundaries, and energy.

Example: "I am a grounded, generous, and wise steward of wealth. I receive easily, circulate joyfully, and create from trust. Money feels safe, and I feel powerful."

Read it daily. Embody it deeply. This becomes your new normal.

Overflow Is the Outcome of Alignment

At the end of your 90-day reset, you won't just feel different—you'll *be* different. You'll have rewired your nervous system, shifted your energy, built new habits, and expanded your identity.

That's how overflow happens.

Not through sudden miracles, but through sustained alignment. Through choices made again and again in the direction of truth.

The reset isn't a finish line—it's a foundation. One you can revisit any time scarcity creeps back in. One you can expand every quarter. One that proves, over and over, that your power to create prosperity lives *within* you.

PART V: BECOMING A CHANNEL

Chapter 17: Wealth Wants to Flow Through You

Most people think of wealth as something to collect. To gather. To hold onto tightly as if it could disappear at any moment. But the truth is, real prosperity isn't stagnant. It isn't something you store—it's something you *channel*. And the moment you stop treating yourself as a container and start embodying the energy of a *conduit*, everything changes.

Wealth wants to move. It wants to circulate, expand, evolve. When you become someone who allows it to flow through you—toward your purpose, your joy, your generosity, your impact—you open the floodgates. The more freely you allow prosperity to move through your life, the more consistently it returns.

This shift in perception—from accumulation to transmission—turns you from someone who chases money into someone who *partners* with it. You become a trusted steward of abundance. A magnet for aligned resources. A source of transformation for others, simply by being who you are and allowing wealth to be what it is: a dynamic, living force.

Let's explore how to make that shift—from fear-based holding to purpose-driven flowing.

Releasing the Fear of Loss

If you've ever hesitated to spend on yourself, delayed investing in your growth, or resisted giving even when you wanted to, chances are you've been trapped in the fear of financial loss. This fear is deeply human. It stems from old survival programming—ancestral experiences of scarcity, childhood moments of lack, societal conditioning that equates spending with danger.

To become a true channel for wealth, you must untangle that fear. You must reframe the belief that when money goes out, you are becoming "less." Because that belief shrinks your energetic field and restricts the very flow you seek to sustain.

Start by remembering this truth: *money is not gone when it is given.* It is activated.

Every time you invest in something aligned, you're not losing—you're planting. Every time you give from joy, you're not depleting—you're expanding your field of trust. Every time you circulate money with intention, you are training your nervous system to see generosity not as a threat but as an expression of overflow.

Here's a practice to start dismantling the fear of loss:
- Before you spend or give, pause and breathe. Ask: "Is this aligned with the version of me who lives in overflow?"
- If yes, spend or give with presence. Say: "This is safe. This is expansion. This is evidence of who I am now."
- Afterward, track what flows back in—not just money, but inspiration, opportunities, clarity, support. Start noticing the reciprocal nature of circulation.

The fear of loss weakens when you witness the law of return in action. The more you allow wealth to move through you without clenching, the more trust you build in the unseen mechanisms of abundance.

The Purpose of Your Prosperity

One of the most empowering questions you can ask on your wealth journey is: *Why does my abundance matter beyond me?* Because when money has purpose, it has power. It moves differently. It finds you more easily. It stays longer. It flows faster. Prosperity that serves only the ego tends to stagnate. But prosperity that serves the soul, the community, or the collective becomes magnetic.

So ask yourself:
- What do I want wealth to *make possible*?
- Who benefits when I thrive?
- What problems can I help solve when I'm resourced?

- How does money amplify my mission, message, or movement?

Your answers don't need to be grand or global. Maybe your purpose is to raise emotionally healthy children. Maybe it's to fund art, or heal others, or open spaces for joy in your community. Maybe it's to show what's possible for people who look like you or came from where you came from.

Your purpose is the why behind your wealth—and when your actions align with that why, you step into a different frequency.

Here's a powerful journaling ritual: Write a letter to Money as if it were a trusted partner. Say, "Here's what I'll do with you when you arrive. Here's how I'll treat you. Here's how we'll work together to create something meaningful."

This isn't about earning worthiness. It's about aligning your intention. When money knows it has a job that feels sacred, it comes with more enthusiasm.

And the best part? You don't have to wait until you have "enough" to start channeling purpose. You can begin now. A small act of service, a donation, an offer shared from your heart, a skill used to help someone—all of these are signs to the universe: *I am ready to be a conduit, not just a consumer.*

Becoming a Safe and Sovereign Channel

To truly let wealth flow through you, you must become someone who can *hold* energy without collapsing, leaking, or overextending. This is where nervous system work, boundaries, and sovereignty come in.

Let's break that down:

1. **Regulate Your Nervous System**

    Money doesn't just flow through your mindset—it flows through your body. If your nervous system perceives receiving as overwhelming, unsafe, or threatening, you will unconsciously block or repel abundance.

To shift this, create daily grounding rituals. Breathe deeply. Anchor into your body. Visualize wealth entering your field while staying relaxed and calm. Teach your system: *It is safe to have more. It is safe to give and receive. I don't have to collapse to be generous.*

2. **Set Energetic and Practical Boundaries**

   Being a channel doesn't mean becoming a martyr. You are not meant to pour until empty. You are meant to circulate from fullness. That means saying no to what drains you, choosing where and how you give, and honoring your own capacity.

If you find yourself overgiving or undercharging, pause and ask: "Is this coming from fear or love? Obligation or overflow?" Real service is sustainable. Real generosity honors you too.

3. **Practice Holding Without Clenching**

   A powerful way to test your capacity as a channel is to receive money—and *not* spend it immediately. Let it sit in your account. Let it live in your wallet. Not because you're hoarding, but because you're *practicing presence*.

Notice any stories that arise: "I should give this away," "I don't deserve this," "It's not safe to keep this." These are echoes of scarcity. Breathe through them. Release them. Choose a new narrative.

Tell yourself: "I am a calm and sovereign steward of wealth. I know when to hold, when to give, and when to invest. I trust myself completely."

When you become this kind of channel—rooted, discerning, generous, and wise—wealth flows through you with ease and consistency. You're no longer chasing money. You've become the place money *loves* to land.

You Were Made for This Flow

Let's be clear: you don't have to be perfect to be a conduit for wealth. You just have to be willing. Willing to look within. Willing to regulate your state. Willing to listen to your deeper purpose. Willing to stay open when your old self wants to shut down.

Wealth wants to flow through you because you're here to *do something with it*. To heal, to liberate, to uplift, to inspire, to shift systems. And you can start now—not someday when you have more, but today, with whatever you already have.

As you continue on this path, remember that you are not just learning how to make money. You are learning how to become someone who *moves* it consciously, courageously, and with deep care.

Chapter 18: How to Receive More Without Guilt or Burnout

Most people think receiving is passive. That it just happens when you've worked hard enough, been good enough, or proven your worth. But that mindset keeps you stuck in cycles of overgiving, overworking, and overcompensating.

Here's the truth: **receiving is an active energetic skill**. And most of us were never taught how to practice it.

From an early age, we learned to value giving. We were praised for helping others, being humble, and putting ourselves last. And while generosity is beautiful, it becomes dysfunctional when it's not balanced with the ability to receive with openness, confidence, and grace.

If you want to experience overflow—true, sustained abundance—you must learn how to receive **without guilt**, **without shrinking**, and **without burning out**.

This chapter will help you do just that. We'll explore the nervous system mechanics of receiving, the emotional patterns that sabotage it, and practical tools to expand your capacity so you can let more in—without falling apart.

Because receiving more isn't just about money. It's about love, help, praise, support, pleasure, rest, joy, and opportunities. When you increase your ability to receive one, you increase your ability to receive all.

Your Nervous System and the Capacity to Hold More

Before you can sustainably receive more in your life, you need to understand the role your nervous system plays in your receptivity. It doesn't matter how much money, love, or opportunity you "manifest" if your system doesn't feel *safe* to hold it.

Your nervous system is designed to keep you alive, not make you rich. Which means when something new enters your life—especially something unfamiliar like overflow—it immediately evaluates: *Is this safe? Is this known? Can I handle this?*

If you've spent most of your life in survival mode—constantly hustling, bracing for the next crisis, or living paycheck to paycheck—then abundance may register as a threat. Not because it's bad, but because it's *different*.

That's why so many people self-sabotage after a financial breakthrough. They get a raise, land a big client, or receive unexpected money—and suddenly they get sick, pick a fight, spend it all, or "forget" to follow through. Their subconscious doesn't know how to hold it.

To expand your receiving capacity, you must regulate your body and **normalize having more**.

Start here:

- **Body Check-In**: Sit quietly and ask yourself, "What happens in my body when I imagine receiving a large amount of money, love, or support?" Notice if you tense up, hold your breath, or feel uneasy. That's your body's resistance.

- **Soothing the Response**: Don't force it away. Instead, breathe into it. Place a hand on your heart or belly. Say, "It's safe to have more. It's safe to receive. Nothing bad is happening."

- **Practice With Small Wins**: Get your system used to saying yes to small things. Accept compliments without deflecting. Say yes when someone offers help. Celebrate when someone thanks or pays you. The more you receive small things openly, the more you prepare your body to handle bigger blessings.

Remember: a nervous system that's calm is a nervous system that can *hold*.

Releasing Guilt and Deservingness Narratives

One of the biggest blocks to receiving is **guilt**—the belief that you haven't done enough to "deserve" what's coming your way. Guilt is a control mechanism. It convinces you that you must earn everything, that you must prove your worth before you're allowed to feel good.

But the truth is, you were born worthy of love, care, and abundance. You don't have to "deserve" wealth in order to receive it—you just have to be willing to align with it.

To receive more, you need to unlearn the guilt that says:
- "Other people have it worse, so I shouldn't want more."
- "I have to suffer first to prove I've earned it."
- "If I receive, someone else has to go without."
- "I'll be judged if I let it be easy."

These thoughts are not moral truths. They're inherited programming—passed down through generations, cultures, and systems designed to keep people small and self-sacrificing.

Let's shift that:
- **You receiving does not take away from others**—it expands what's possible for everyone.
- **You resting, thriving, or earning easily** doesn't make you bad—it makes you a model of aligned living.
- **You having more** allows you to circulate more, give more, support more, and create more.

Guilt is a signal that your identity is bumping into your expansion. When that happens, breathe. Don't retreat. Reframe. Say:

"I am allowed to receive. My joy does not harm others. My abundance serves the whole."

One powerful exercise: every time you receive something—a compliment, a payment, a gift—pause and say aloud, "I receive this fully." Let the words land. Practice until it feels normal.

You are not stealing oxygen by thriving. You are setting an example of what's possible when people live in alignment with truth and love.

Creating Systems That Support Overflow

Once you've begun expanding your nervous system and releasing guilt, the final piece is creating **structures and practices that**

support your new capacity. Because receiving without containers leads to leaks. And leaks create exhaustion.

Here's how to stabilize and sustain your new level of abundance:

1. **Create a Prosperity Schedule**

    Most burnout doesn't come from "too much abundance"—it comes from having no boundaries around the abundance. More clients, more money, more attention—these are gifts, but they need structure.

Create a weekly or daily rhythm that includes rest, integration, and energetic recalibration. Protect your time. Say no often. Let your calendar reflect the truth that your energy is your most precious currency.

2. **Build Overflow Reserves**

    As your income or opportunities increase, don't rush to spend or give it all away. Allow yourself to hold. Create buffers in your bank account. Build an "abundance reserve" fund. Let overflow be *normal*—not something to eliminate immediately through guilt or pressure.

Practice holding without urgency. This tells your system: "We are safe to have. We are safe to wait. We are no longer in survival."

3. **Ritualize Receiving**

    Make receiving sacred. Every time money or goodness enters your life, pause to acknowledge it. Light a candle. Speak gratitude. Journal how it makes you feel. This anchors the experience as *real* in your subconscious.

The more you ritualize receiving, the more your brain says, "This is who we are now." And your life will rise to meet that identity.

4. **Celebrate Without Collapse**

    Sometimes after a big win, we unconsciously collapse. We get sick, isolate, or sabotage. To avoid this, create a post-receiving ritual. After every up-level, ask:

- How do I want to honor this moment?
- How can I rest and integrate this expansion?
- What does this mean about who I'm becoming?

Give yourself space to absorb what you've created. Let the celebration be a bridge to the next level—not a cliff.

Receiving Is the Beginning, Not the End

Ultimately, learning how to receive without guilt or burnout is the bridge between survival and sustainability. It's the space where you stop chasing and start allowing. Where you stop clenching and start creating. Where you stop just hoping for abundance and start living in it.

When you master the art of receiving:
- You no longer doubt your worth—you embody it.
- You no longer fear the next breakthrough—you *prepare* for it.
- You no longer shrink when blessings arrive—you rise to meet them.

This is your invitation to let it be easier. To let it be enough. To hold more, with grace. And to know that you are capable of doing so, not because you've earned it—but because you are aligned with it.

Chapter 19: Prosperity & Purpose – Aligning Money with Meaning

We live in a world where people chase wealth as a standalone goal. Make six figures. Become a millionaire. Hit that seven-figure launch. Yet, how many of those people—once they "arrive"—feel empty, burned out, or misaligned?

That's because wealth without purpose is like a powerful river with no direction. It flows, yes—but aimlessly. It erodes rather than builds. It can drown the soul rather than elevate it.

Real prosperity isn't just having more—it's knowing why you have it, how you're meant to use it, and how it serves something greater than accumulation. Meaning is what transforms money from a tool into a mission.

When your prosperity is aligned with your purpose, you stop second-guessing your value. You no longer chase dollars—you steward vision. You no longer compete for success—you amplify what's uniquely yours to give.

Purpose turns your wealth into a force of impact, joy, and legacy. Without it, you'll always wonder if it's enough. With it, even a modest income can feel like divine abundance.

Let's unpack how to discover, align with, and build from the powerful intersection of money and meaning.

Discovering Your Unique Purpose

Purpose isn't a job title. It's not a business model or a personal brand. It's a deeper orientation—an expression of your soul's essence, your unique perspective, your lived experiences, and the transformation you're here to embody and offer.

You don't find your purpose by thinking your way into it. You uncover it by noticing the themes that have always moved you. The problems you feel called to solve. The stories you can't stop telling. The people you long to serve or represent.

Here are questions to help you excavate your purpose:
- What pain have I turned into wisdom?

- What topic could I speak about for hours without preparation?
- Who do I naturally attract—and what do they come to me for?
- When do I feel most alive, most electric, most myself?
- What injustice or gap in the world breaks my heart to witness?

Often, purpose hides in plain sight. It shows up in your conversations, your curiosities, the compliments you brush off. It's what you do when no one is watching. It's how you make people feel without trying.

And contrary to what many believe, you don't need to monetize your purpose directly to be aligned. A day job can serve your purpose if it funds your art. A business can serve your purpose if it reflects your values. Parenting can be purpose. Teaching can be purpose. Beauty, joy, humor, and storytelling can all be sacred forms of purpose.

The key is this: your prosperity feels meaningful when you can trace its source to something *real* inside you—and when you can see how it ripples outward into lives beyond your own.

Bridging Money and Meaning in Daily Life

Once you've touched into your sense of purpose, the next step is building a tangible bridge between that inner compass and your external prosperity. This doesn't require massive change. It starts with small, consistent alignment.

Here's how to begin aligning money with meaning:

1. **Audit Your Current Streams of Income**

    Look at how you currently earn money. Ask:
    - Does this work reflect my values?
    - Do I feel proud of how this money is made?
    - Am I compromising my purpose for stability, or is this income serving my bigger mission?

You don't need to quit your job or overhaul your business tomorrow. But awareness opens the door to intentional evolution. Maybe you shift your messaging. Maybe you adjust your pricing. Maybe you create a new offer that lights you up.

2. **Infuse Your Work With Your Why**

    Even if you're not in your "dream job," you can bring purpose into how you do what you do. Infuse conversations with kindness. Bring more creativity into routine tasks. Speak truth even when it's inconvenient. Create with care.

When you remember why you're doing something—not just for a paycheck but for your legacy—you energize your actions. Clients, customers, coworkers, and collaborators feel that. And prosperity responds to that resonance.

3. **Spend and Give in Alignment**

    Aligning money with meaning also means looking at where your money goes. Are you spending in ways that reflect your values? Are you supporting businesses, creators, causes, or communities you believe in?

Are you giving—not just out of obligation, but as an act of expression?

Try this: the next time you buy something, ask, "Does this purchase support the world I want to live in?" When you give, say, "This gift is an extension of my purpose." Watch how your relationship with money deepens.

4. **Declare a Prosperity Mission Statement**

    Write a short statement that clarifies how you want your wealth to serve your purpose.

Example: "I create money with ease so I can build safe spaces for marginalized voices." Or, "My income funds my art and allows me to raise my children in joy and freedom." Or, "I prosper so that I can teach others to thrive beyond trauma."

This statement becomes your compass. When you feel lost, guilty, or confused about money, return to it.

Purpose is not static. It will evolve. But if you keep anchoring your money choices to meaning, you'll never feel disconnected from your soul.

Purpose-Driven Wealth is Sustainable and Expansive

When your money is rooted in your mission, you stop treating prosperity as a finite goal. You see it as an ecosystem. An unfolding.

You make decisions not just for today's survival, but for tomorrow's expansion. You invest in your capacity, your education, your tools—not to prove something, but because your mission matters.

You become more resilient to failure. Because even when a launch flops or a contract ends, your *why* remains. You recalibrate. You re-choose. You remember who you are.

You also stop playing small. When you know your money matters to more than just your ego, you take bolder actions. You charge what you're worth. You say yes to visibility. You hire help. You show up when it's inconvenient—because you're not doing this *for* money. You're doing this *with* money.

You treat money not as a god or a goal, but as a partner in your soul's work.

And finally, your wealth becomes a transmission. People feel it. They don't just buy your offer or support your brand—they buy into your *belief* in something better. They feel safe around your leadership. They trust your generosity. They rise with your overflow.

This is legacy. This is energetic impact. This is the deeper truth: your prosperity was never just about you. It was always about what could move *through* you.

As we move into the final chapter, you'll learn how to lock in this alignment so that prosperity becomes not a peak, but a *default state*—one you live in, expand from, and teach by example.

Let's close the loop. Let's seal the code. Let's step fully into the invisible identity of the truly abundant.

Chapter 20: The Invisible Code of the Truly Abundant

What separates those who occasionally "get lucky" with money from those who live in a continual state of abundance? It's not intelligence, strategy, or even circumstance. It's embodiment.

The truly abundant have tapped into an invisible code—one that governs their decisions, their energy, their expectations, and their identity. This code isn't written in financial ledgers or business plans. It's encoded in how they *be*. How they show up when no one is watching. How they respond to setbacks. How they regulate their emotions, trust their path, and walk with inner certainty long before evidence appears.

This invisible code is a lived frequency. It's the set of energetic agreements that define a person's relationship with flow, receiving, and generosity. When you live by it, prosperity becomes your atmosphere—not your achievement. You stop chasing abundance and start transmitting it.

In this chapter, we'll decode the key traits, habits, and inner agreements of those who live in sustained overflow—not because they "figured it out," but because they became *someone different* on a cellular level.

Let's walk through what that looks like in practice.

Abundant People Trust Before They See

One of the first hallmarks of truly abundant individuals is that they operate from a place of deep, embodied trust. They don't wait for outer results to feel secure—they generate that safety from within.

This doesn't mean they're naive or reckless. Quite the opposite. It means they've trained themselves to see reality not only as it is, but as it's becoming. They're vision-driven, not evidence-dependent.

They ask themselves:
- "What story am I choosing to live into right now?"

- "How would I act today if I trusted the outcome was guaranteed?"
- "How can I anchor into safety even in uncertainty?"

This trust creates momentum. Because when you're no longer waiting for proof before you move, you create the very evidence you used to need.

In contrast, people stuck in scarcity often live in reaction. They wait to feel good until they see results. They try to "earn" clarity through overthinking. They demand control because they don't feel safe without guarantees.

Abundant people live differently. They allow movement to create clarity. They understand that the universe responds to faith in action. They show up *as if*—not because they're faking it, but because they're building reality from the inside out.

You can cultivate this too. Start each day asking: *What version of me am I rehearsing today? Who do I need to become to match the life I want?* Then move from that identity, even if the outer world hasn't caught up yet.

Abundant People Circulate Without Fear

Another powerful aspect of the invisible code is circulation. Abundant people understand that wealth is not something to hoard—it's something to *move*. They aren't afraid to spend, invest, or give, because they know they are connected to a source greater than any transaction.

This doesn't mean they're careless or impulsive. It means they know that clenching breeds stagnation. They trust the law of return. They know that when money flows out in alignment, it creates space for something greater to return.

They ask questions like:
- "Where does this money want to go next?"
- "How can I use this payment as a portal to expansion?"
- "Am I spending from fear or from embodiment?"

Scarcity-based mindsets often approach money with the energy of emergency. Even when funds are available, they panic. They say no to opportunity, support, or even pleasure—because they're still playing the game of survival, even in seasons of growth.

Truly abundant people have shifted that. They know how to circulate without collapsing. They know how to give without draining. They know how to hold wealth with both gratitude and detachment.

One way to embody this trait: Create a weekly or monthly ritual where you consciously move money—whether that's paying a bill with reverence, tipping generously, donating, or investing in your capacity. Speak to the money as it leaves: "Thank you for circulating. Return multiplied."

This teaches your subconscious: I am the source, not the bucket. I am connected to the infinite.

Abundant People Let Identity Lead Everything

Perhaps the most foundational element of the invisible code is this: abundant people live from identity, not outcomes. They don't wait to *become* wealthy after they have wealth—they become wealthy *before* the wealth arrives.

This means they make decisions based on who they've chosen to be, not what they currently have.

They ask:
- "What would the version of me who lives in overflow do here?"
- "What boundaries does my abundant self enforce?"
- "What environment does she create for herself?"
- "What thoughts does he no longer entertain?"

This isn't "fake it till you make it." It's *embody it until it matches*. It's identity-first living. Because when your self-concept shifts, your actions shift. And when your actions shift, your outcomes follow.

Abundant people treat this identity like sacred soil. They guard it. They nourish it. They keep it clean from energy leaks, from gossip, from scarcity conversations, from environments that shrink them.

They dress for the life they're stepping into. They speak with clarity and conviction. They honor their time like it matters. They create before they're asked. They choose alignment over approval. They invest before they're fully ready—not recklessly, but *faithfully*.

They don't just set boundaries—they embody standards.

And here's the truth: this identity isn't about arrogance or perfection. It's about resonance. It's about becoming so familiar with your next-level self that it becomes harder to *not* be them.

You don't step into abundance by wishing. You step into it by becoming. Daily. Deliberately.

Sealing the Code: From Knowledge to Integration

You've made it to the final chapter of this book—but in truth, this is the beginning of your embodiment.

Throughout these pages, you've uncovered the laws behind true prosperity. You've questioned myths, recoded your field, built habits, and learned to circulate. You've seen that wealth is not a number, but a state. Not a possession, but a frequency. Not a goal, but a mirror.

Now, the work becomes one of **integration**. Of not just knowing, but *living*. Of becoming fluent in the invisible language of expansion—until it's your first tongue.

To seal this, ask yourself:
- What have I outgrown energetically?
- What rituals or boundaries must now become non-negotiable?
- What version of me have I been rehearsing—and who am I now claiming to be?

Write these answers. Declare them. Practice them. Share them.

Because the truly abundant don't just shift for themselves. They shift for those around them. They create ripple effects of permission, of possibility, of liberation.

This is how we change culture. Not by preaching prosperity—but by *embodying* it, quietly, consistently, boldly.

You now carry the code.

May you walk with it, live with it, share it—and watch as the world reflects it back to you, tenfold.

www.ingramcontent.com/pod-product-compliance
Lightning Source LLC
Chambersburg PA
CBHW072159160426

43197CB00012B/2457